W9-ALZ-944

Illustrators:
Larry Bauer
Keith Vasconcelles

Editor:
Karen Goldfluss, M.S. Ed.

Editor-in-Chief:
Sharon Coan, M.S. Ed.

Art Director:
Elayne Roberts

Cover Artist:
Keith Vasconcelles

Product Manager:
Phil Garcia

Imaging:
Hillary Merriman

Publishers:
Rachelle Cracchiolo, M.S. Ed.
Mary Dupuy Smith, M.S. Ed.

Portfolio Planner

A Step-By-Step Guide to Portfolio Assessment

Author:

Julia Jasmine, M.A.

Teacher Created Materials, Inc.
P.O. Box 1040
Huntington Beach, CA   92647
©1995 Teacher Created Materials, Inc.
Made in U.S.A.
ISBN-1-55734-546-5

The classroom teacher may reproduce copies of materials in this book for classroom use only. The reproduction of any part for an entire school or school system is strictly prohibited. No part of this publication may be transmitted, stored, or recorded in any form without written permission from the publisher.

Table of Contents

Introduction

If you are a teacher who is looking for a user-tested, prepackaged, step-by-step portfolio assessment method, this is for you.

If you have read all of the other books and attended what seems like every single one of the inservice workshops and training sessions that have ever been offered, this is your book.

If you have listened to more than enough experts and tried to put all of their often-contradictory advice into action in your classroom, read this.

If you have felt bogged down and considered giving up the whole idea—somewhere between the first paper misfiled by a student and the realization that you must, somehow or other, pull together all of the information you have gathered and use it to assign grades—here is help.

In other words, if you are the one over there in the corner of your classroom, screaming and tearing out your hair, everything is going to be okay!

Portfolio assessment can be a snap if you first take a deep breath and then take the portfolio process step by step.

Start Here

1. Read "Basic Premises for Portfolio Assessment" and "Most Important of All" below.

2. Then read the "Overview" of the Seven Steps and the elaboration of each of the steps.

3. The "Planning" step will show you how to put this simplified and streamlined system of portfolio assessment into action for yourself.

Basic Premises for Portfolio Assessment

One of the very first things you will need to do when you start portfolio assessment is to decide where to put everything. But even before you do that, you will find it helpful to accept a few basic premises:

❖ Your first working portfolios (referred to as Collection Portfolios, Accumulation Portfolios, Initial Portfolios, or just drop files) will not be pretty.

❖ Nothing about the beginning stages of portfolio assessment can be considered neat or tidy.

❖ Showcase Portfolios (the tidy, organized ones) are used later in the "Showcasing" stage.

Most Important of All

Once you have accepted these premises, which are difficult for many teachers to accept, you need to know only one other thing before you start. This is the single most important piece of information in this book.

Every piece of paper that goes into a portfolio must be dated!

Overview

Step One: Storage

Make a container, anything from a folded piece of construction paper to a sturdy cardboard box, for each student and label it with his or her name. These are your Collection Portfolios. (You can call them your Accumulation or Initial Portfolios, or even your drop files, if that makes you more comfortable.)

Put these containers in an area of your classroom that is accessible to both you and the students. See more about "Storage" on page 6.

Step Two: Contents

Decide what you want to keep. You may decide to keep all writing samples, all the work done in the area of a specific theme, or a weekly sample of work from each area of the curriculum. In addition, you may want to include elaborated student work samples, such as reflections, peer editing, reading and writing logs, and so on. You may want to collect your own anecdotal records and contracts in the Collection Portfolios, too. See the description on page 8.

Step Three: Filing

Set up your system for filing. Each student might be responsible for getting his or her own papers into the portfolio, or a student Portfolio Aide might be responsible for filing everything.

If you decide to have a Portfolio Aide, make sure he or she trains a backup. Even Portfolio Aides get sick (or need a day off) and papers pile up quickly. See more information about filing on page 100.

Overview *(cont.)*

Step Four: Sorting

Choose your showcase samples by having students sort through the papers in their Collection Portfolios. The time to do this might be at the end of a short unit, at a good stopping point in a longer unit, or right before parent conferences.

Distribute the portfolios and have the students choose papers according to criteria that suit your purpose. (See page 103.)

Step Five: Showcasing

Move the selected papers into the Showcase Portfolios. The remaining papers should be sent home and the now empty Collection Portfolios returned to the accessible area so you and the students can start the collection process all over again.

Now is the time to make a Showcase Portfolio container. This is your opportunity to be artistic and creative. The students will love it. You will find some ideas to use on page 123.

Step Six: Uses

Use the contents of the portfolios

    ...to assess student progress.

    ...as an end-of-the-year display at Open House.

    ...as a record of progress to be sent home at year's end.

    ...as a technique for encouraging students to take ownership of their learning process. (See page 139.)

Step Seven: Planning

After you have read through the first six steps and before you really start the process, this last step will show you how to use a blank calendar of your school year to plan your portfolio assessment system every step of the way. (See page 141.)

Step One of the Portfolio Planner

Just a Reminder

Your first portfolios will be working portfolios, designed to collect the materials needed to set the system in motion and help you control the paper avalanche. You will be collecting samples of student work in them, but you do not have to collect everything. Feel free to send some things home. This will keep parents informed and give you more space in the classroom.

Make a Container

In order to actually get started, simply make a container for each student and label it with his or her name. These containers can be anything from folded pieces of construction paper to sturdy boxes. Your choice, which may change after you try it out, will depend on

...the size of the work samples you will be asking students to collect and save.

...the space you have available to store these containers.

...the amount of money you are able to spend.

Commercially Available Products

Commercially available products are very satisfactory. By all means, use them if you can afford them. Manila folders in either letter size or legal size are easy to use. Hanging folders in sizes to match your folders make them even easier. (Consider investing in these, even if you cannot afford to buy anything else. They keep slippery file folders, even those made of construction paper, upright and keep them from sliding down underneath everything.

Storing Large Objects

If you are teaching very young children who use very large paper for their products, consider folding things for storage because large portfolios are very difficult to store. Another option is to reduce the large product with a copier, send home the original for parents to treasure, and store the reduced copy in the child's portfolio.

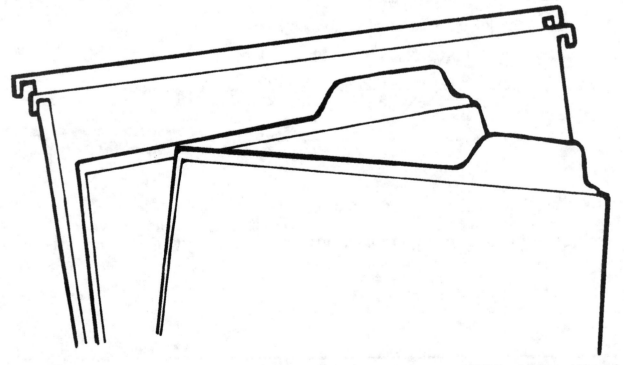

6 ©*1995 Teacher Created Materials, Inc.*

Step One of the Portfolio Planner *(cont.)*

Store the Containers

Crates and boxes are available to accommodate all of the filing devices described on page 6. Publishers often send their teachers' editions in file-size plastic crates that can be used for portfolio storage. Many stores, especially office supply stores, carry boxes that are designed for storage. They carry heavy cardboard boxes called "bankers' boxes." These come flat, and you fold and assemble them yourself. Buy the ones that are constructed to accept letter-size files one way and legal-size files the other.

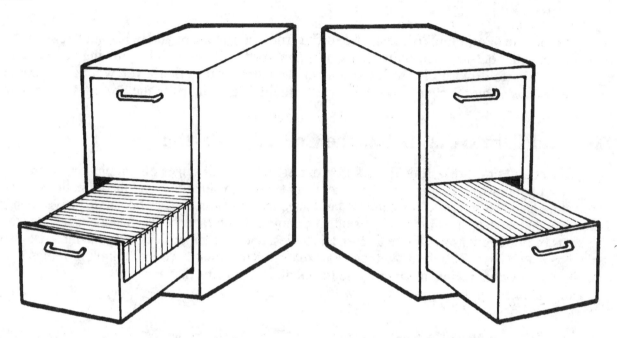

Regular file cabinets are often part of the standard furniture found in a classroom. They will either accept hanging folders or can be adapted for them with the addition of brackets that fit inside the drawers. If you have enough of them, file cabinets are superb places to keep portfolios because you can use the bottom drawers, leave them pulled out for work time, and close them up out of sight when you want the room to look neat.

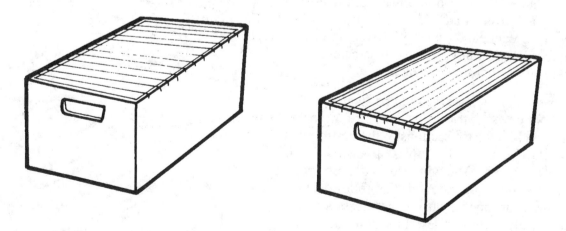

While you and your students are using these working portfolios for the day-to-day collection of their work samples, the students can start early to create elegant, personalized portfolio covers to hold the materials that will make up their Showcase Portfolios—the end result of sorting through this paper blizzard.

Make a List

So, what will you include in your portfolios? Make one or more lists, depending on your purpose in having portfolios to begin with. Remember, with the exception of lists of requirements mandated by your district or by a school administrator, you can always change your mind about what to put in your portfolios. You can add to and delete from the lists. You can even start over with an entirely new list. It is up to you.

Portfolio Wish List

Your own private "Portfolio Wish List" may differ from the statement you will want to post on the front cover (either outside or inside) of the Collection Portfolios that will be growing before your very eyes. Your "Portfolio Wish List" will probably be the basis for the criteria you will use to choose papers for showcasing. Sample lists to help you with this are included in the Sorting section of this book.

Lists and Forms That Define the Collection Portfolio

Your Collection Portfolios will hold work in progress, work in all stages of completion, work waiting to be reflected upon, work waiting for peer review and teacher evaluation—and the reflections, reviews, and evaluations themselves. They can also hold anecdotal records, lists of books that have been read, and pieces that have been written by the students, copies of contracts between students and teachers, checklists of observations in science and social studies, and a lot more, including the materials the students want to save. This is certainly not an exhaustive inventory. You will think of things that are necessary for your individual program. Use (or modify) the forms that are listed and supplied on the pages that follow to help you with all of these inclusions.

Since working portfolios must be accessible to students in order to be useful, they also become accessible to everyone who comes into your classroom. The "Collection Portfolio Statement," which identifies the portfolio as a "collection" or "working" portfolio and gives a brief description of what might be found inside, can be stapled to the outside front cover of a Collection Portfolio. It will save you a great deal of time by explaining the portfolio to classroom visitors such as parents, administrators, and/or other teachers.

Another type of list, one that can be stapled to the inside front cover of the Collection Portfolio or used as dividers for the sections of the portfolio, is the "Work Inventory." Examples of general lists of this type are given. You will also find more specific lists in the subject-area sections that follow. This type of list is as much a work in progress as is the portfolio itself. Titles or descriptions of the work samples can be added to these lists—written in by you or the students—when the pieces are filed in the portfolios. This will help you and your students when it is time to sort through the collection for one

The Mandated List

Teachers may find themselves using a mandated portfolio assessment approach for a variety of reasons. In many cases, they may have accepted or even requested it as an alternative to the traditional report card.

In some ways the mandated portfolio is the easiest one to implement. It does not require selection of material in response to instruction. (In fact, it will probably require instruction in response to the list of required work samples.)

Keep the following information in mind if your district or school administration has mandated portfolio assessment.

- The portfolios will almost assuredly be used to assess student progress and may be used to compare classrooms and/or schools.

- Portfolios may be used to assess your performance as a teacher.

- The contents of the portfolios will probably determine, at least in part, report card grades, so parents will also be involved in the portfolio process.

- Portfolios may be passed on, in whole or in part, to the next teacher.

If the contents of your portfolios are mandated by your district or school administration, you should obtain all the guidelines concerning

…the kind of containers in which to store items.

…the samples you must collect.

Learn all you can about how the portfolios will be used for students assessment, who owns them, whether or not they will follow the students, and what your own accountability will be.

Since these will be official district or school assessment tools, be just as careful about what you include in them as you are about what you include in the cumulative folders. Consider keeping more than one kind of portfolio for each student.

Although the mandated portfolio is not a Collection Portfolio, a "Statement for the Mandated Portfolio" is provided in the section containing general forms. If you are not provided with a special form, use it to list the samples you are required to keep.

Most of the forms that follow appear in different styles and in versions appropriate for different grade levels. Browse through them to find the ones that are right for you, or adapt them to suit your own purposes.

As you think about lists and forms, consider color coding them. If, for example, you run all the anecdotal records on blue, you can pull them when the Collection Portfolios are sorted and put them aside (or put them back in what will then be empty folders) to help you when you are making decisions about grades. Or, if you run all the reflection forms on another color, you can take a quick look at that area of a student's work without leafing through every paper in the portfolio.

The following forms can be found on pages 11 through 22.

 ©1995 *Teacher Created Materials, Inc.*

Collection Portfolio Statement 1

The statement that appears below describes the Collection Portfolio so that parents and other visitors will have a general idea of your purpose and of the students' success. It can be attached to the outside front cover of the portfolio.

The Collection Portfolio

The pieces collected in this portfolio are representative samples of the ongoing work of this student in this classroom. Each piece has some significance in some area of the curriculum. The pieces are not in any particular order, but they are dated so that progress can be observed when they are put in chronological order.

The papers you will find here will fall into these and other categories:

☞ writing samples

☞ journal entries

☞ reading responses and checklists

☞ problems and solutions in math

☞ reports in social studies

☞ records of science investigations

☞ important tests

If you would like to know more about a particular piece, please ask either the student or the teacher. We would appreciate your positive remarks about the work you observe.

_____
Teacher

_____
Student

Collection Portfolio Statement 2

The statement that appears below describes the Collection Portfolio so that parents and other visitors will have a general idea of your purpose and of the student's success. It can be attached to the outside front cover of the portfolio.

This Collection Portfolio belongs to _____

It contains samples of my work in these subject areas:

❏ **Mathematics**

❏ **Writing**

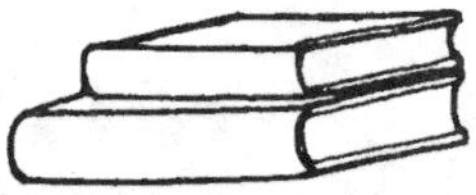

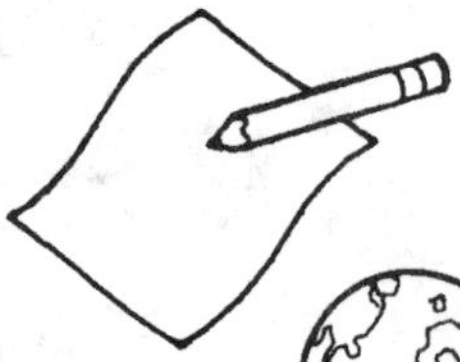

❏ **Social Studies**

❏ **Science**

❏ **Art/Music**

❏ **Other**

Collection Portfolio Statement 3

If no special form is provided, you can complete this Mandated Portfolio Form, or a variation of it, and attach a copy to the front cover of a portfolio containing the work samples mandated by your district or school.

This Portfolio reflects the academic progress of

_____

It contains work samples meeting mandated requirements
in these subject areas:

Attach a copy of this general form, or a variation of it, to the inside front cover of each Collection Portfolio to indicate the portfolio's contents. Save yourself hours of explanation by having students check categories and list pieces of work as they place them in the portfolios.

This Collection Portfolio is the property of

_____

It contains samples of my work in these subject areas:

☐ Writing

_____

_____

_____

☐ Math

_____

_____

_____

☐ Social Studies

_____

_____

_____

☐ Science

_____

_____

_____

☐ Art/Music

_____

_____

_____

Anecdotal Records—Form 1

Reproduce some of these classroom lists and carry them around on a clipboard to make moment-by-moment comments on what you observe in your classroom. Transfer the information to individual record forms at the end of the day.

Record of Observed Behavior

Date	Child's Name	Comment

Anecdotal Records—Form 2

Make several copies of this form and carry them around on a clipboard to make moment-by-moment comments on what you observe in your classroom. Transfer the comments to individual record forms at the end of the day. Elaborate as desired.

Record of Observed Behavior

DATE	STUDENT'S NAME	COMMENT

Individual Anecdotal Records—Form 1

Duplicate this form and use it for keeping your own anecdotal records.

✍ Anecdotal Record Form ✍

Date _____

Student's Name _____

Subject _____

Instructional Situation _____

Instructional Task _____

Behavior Observed _____

_____

_____

_____

_____

_____

This behavior was important because_____

_____

_____

_____

_____

_____

Reproduce a stack of these forms and keep them — one for each student in your class — in a three-ring binder. Make your notes on the appropriate form. When a page is filled replace it with a new page. Add the completed page to the student's portfolio. No time is lost transcribing information!

Individual Anecdotal Record

Name _____

Date	Comment

Individual Anecdotal Records—Form 3

Reproduce several copies of this form and keep them — one for each student in your class — in a three-ring binder. Make your notes on the appropriate form. When a page is filled replace it with a new page. Add the completed page to the student's portfolio. No time is lost transcribing information!

Individual Anecdotal Record

Name _____

Date	Comment

This form is designed to introduce the primary student to the idea of the contract. Agreement can be reached orally and specific assignments written in by the teacher during a conference with the student.

CONTRACT
Primary

I have just finished _____

_____.

The next thing I will do in _____

is _____

_____.

I will have this done by my next conference on _____

_____.

_____
Student

_____
Date

Contract Form—Upper Grade

This form is designed to help the teacher use student conferencing time to its best advantage by having the student make a definite commitment to his or her next steps in the learning process.

CONTRACT
Upper Grade

Having just completed _____

_____,

my next steps in the area of _____

are _____

_____

_____

_____.

I agree to complete these assignments by _____

which is the date of my next conference.

_____
Student

_____
Date

Contract Form—Advanced

This form is designed to help the teacher use student conferencing time to its best advantage by having the student make a definite commitment to his or her next steps in the learning process.

Contract

Having just completed _____

_____

my next steps in the area of _____

are _____

_____

_____

_____

_____ .

I agree to complete these assignments by _____

which is the date of my next conference.

_____   _____
Student   *Date*

Language Arts

Forms for Collecting Information

Student Reading Record—Primary

Make copies of this form for your students. They can use them at home and when completed return them to place in their portfolios. Students can also keep them in their portfolios and update them when they finish a book. Or they can have two at a time — one for home use and one for school use. Parents can verify home reading by initialing the book entry. Decide on a quick rating system — maybe one to five stars or happy faces. Children love to rate their reading.

Books I Have Read

Name _____

Date turned in _____

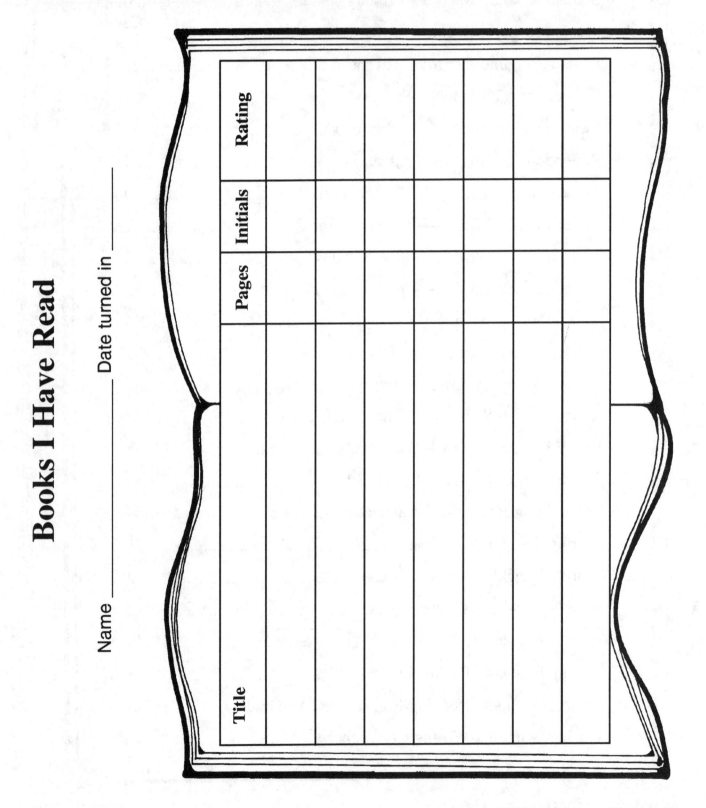

Title	Pages	Initials	Rating

Student Reading Record—Upper Grade

Make copies of this form for your students. They can use them at home and return them when completed to place in their portfolios. Or students can keep them in their portfolios and update them when they finish a book.

Student Reading Record
UPPER GRADE

Name _____

Date	Title of Book	# of pages	Response to Book (written or oral report, other)

Make copies of this form for your students. They can use them at home and return them when completed to place in their portfolios. Or, students can keep them in their portfolios and update them when they finish a book. You may wish to have students keep two records at a time — one for home use and one for school use. Decide on a quick rating system, such as one to five stars.

Book List

Name _____

TITLE	AUTHOR	DATE	RATING/ RESPONSE

Reflections on Reading—Primary

Make copies of this form for your students to use as they start the process of reflecting on their own progress in reading. This particular form was designed for primary children and requires little writing. A teacher—student conference affords a good time to start reflecting on progress in reading. At that time the teacher can help the student fill in the name of the book he or she was reading at the beginning of the year.

Reflections on Reading

Name _____ Date _____

At the beginning of the year, I was reading _____.

Now I am reading _____.

This is how I feel about my progress in reading *(circle one)*:

happy   not sure   sad

I am really proud of _____

_____

_____

_____

The next book I plan to read is _____

_____

Reflections on Reading—Upper Grade

Make copies of this form for your students to use as they start the process of reflecting on their own progress in reading. Teacher—student conferences afford a good opportunity for this. At that time the teacher can help the students decide on the books they will read next.

Reflections on Reading

Name _____   Date _____

At the beginning of the year I was reading _____

_____.

Now I am reading _____

_____.

When I look at the difference in what I can read now, I feel _____

_____.

Now I can _____

_____.

I am really proud of _____

_____.

The next book I plan to read is _____

_____

because _____

_____.

Reflections on Reading—Advanced

You can reproduce this form for your students to use to reflect on the books they read during the school year.

Book Review

Name _____ Date _____

Title _____

Author _____

Illustrator _____

Number of Pages _____

✦ ✦ ✦ ✦ ✦

Write a short summary of the book.

_____

_____

_____

_____

_____

_____

_____

✦ ✦ ✦ ✦ ✦

Reflect on your response to the book.

_____

_____

_____

_____

_____

_____

_____

Reflections on Writing—Primary

Make copies of this form for your students to use as they start the process of reflecting on their own writing. This form was designed for primary children and requires little writing. If your students need a more sophisticated form, use the one on page 31. Allow plenty of time to look over the work that is being reflected upon. When the form is completed, attach it to the work and include it in the student's portfolio.

Reflections on Writing

Name_____ Date _____

When I look back at the work I have done, I feel

I have become better in

writing sentences.

using capitals and periods.

spelling.

telling a story.

telling my ideas about something.

I am really proud of

_____

_____.

The next time I write I will

_____

_____.

This form is designed to introduce the idea of reflecting on a piece of one's own writing to the primary student. The ideas may be shared orally with the teacher who can fill in the information.

Reflecting on Writing

Name_____ Date _____

Title of piece_____

I want this piece in my portfolio because _____

_____

_____

_____

_____.

My favorite sentence is _____

_____

_____

_____

_____.

Reflections on Writing—Upper Grade

Make copies of this form for your students to use as they start the process of reflecting on their own writing. (Although this form was designed for upper grade children, it could be used by younger children if the teacher reads it to them and briefly records their answers. Some primary students may, of course, be ready to use it alone.) Allow plenty of time to look over the work that is being reflected upon. When the form is completed, attach it to the work and include it in the student's portfolio.

Reflections on Writing

Name_____ Date _____

When I look back at the work I have done, I feel _____

_____

_____

_____.

I have become better in/at _____

_____

_____

_____.

I am really proud of _____

_____

_____

_____.

The next time I write, I will work on _____

_____

_____.

32 ©1995 Teacher Created Materials, Inc.

Reflections on Writing—Upper Grade *(cont.)*

This form is designed to assist students in reflecting on pieces of their own writing. Since reflecting on a piece of writing means taking a thoughtful look at it, a form is not the ideal vehicle. Nevertheless, since some students find this process threatening, a form may introduce the idea without creating a stressful writing situation. There will be time enough later to require the reflective essay.

Reflecting on Writing

Name_____ Date _____

Title of piece _____

I chose this piece because _____

_____

_____.

Its special strengths are _____

_____

_____.

If I were going to redo this piece now, I would _____

_____

_____

_____.

This form is designed to assist students in reflecting on single pieces of their own writing. Since reflecting on a piece of writing means looking at it in order to make a thoughtful response to it, a form is not the ideal vehicle. Nevertheless, since some students find the reflective process threatening at first, a form can introduce the idea without creating a stressful writing situation. There will be enough time later to require a reflective essay, such as the one on page 35.

Reflecting on Writing

Name_____ Date _____

Title of piece _____

I chose to reflect on this piece because _____

_____

_____.

Its special strengths are _____

_____

_____.

In my next piece, I plan to work on _____

_____

_____

_____

_____.

The Reflective Essay—Advanced

Student Writing Sample

Name_____ Date _____

Writing Situation

Soon you will be a freshman in high school. This will be a big change, but you can probably predict what it will be like and how you will feel because of other experiences you have had.

Directions for Writing

Write an essay describing how you think you will feel as a freshman in high school. What life experiences can you draw on to help you picture this? Describe at least one of these experiences and explain how it helps. Use correct grammar, punctuation, and spelling.

_____

_____

_____

_____

_____

_____

_____

_____

_____

_____

_____

_____

_____

_____

_____

_____

_____

_____

_____

_____

_____

_____

Make copies of this form for your students to use as they start the process of reflecting on their own progress in spelling. Spelling — especially invented or estimated (phonetic) spelling — is being mentioned more and more often as an indicator of a student's control of the language. This form was designed for primary students and requires little writing. A teacher—student conference affords an opportunity to start reflecting on progress in spelling.

Reflections on Spelling

Name _____ Date_____

This is how I feel about my progress in spelling (circle one):

I have learned to spell many words the way they are spelled in books.

Here are some words I can spell:

_____   _____   _____

_____   _____   _____

_____   _____   _____

When I don't know how to spell a word, I can _____

_____

_____.

It is fun to be able to spell because _____

_____.

Reflections on Spelling—Upper Grade

Make copies of this form for your students to use as they start the process of reflecting on their own progress in spelling. Spelling — especially invented or estimated (phonetic) spelling — is being mentioned more and more often as an indicator of a student's control of the language. A teacher/student conference affords an opportunity to start reflecting on progress in spelling.

Reflections on Spelling

Name_____ Date _____

When I compare my spelling at the beginning of the year to my spelling now, I see that I have learned to spell many more words correctly. Here are some words I can spell.

_____   _____   _____

_____   _____   _____

_____   _____   _____

When I don't know how to spell a word, I can_____

_____

_____

_____.

It is important to know how to sound out words because

_____

_____.

It is important to learn conventional spelling because

_____

_____.

This form is designed to introduce the primary student to the idea of peer editing. Opinions can be given orally and written by the teacher.

Peer Editing Response
Primary

The piece I read was _____

by _____ .

The best thing about this piece is _____

_____

_____ .

It would be even better if _____

_____

_____

_____ .

_____   _____
Peer Editor   *Date*

Peer Editing Response—Upper Grade

This form is designed to facilitate and formalize the peer editing process. Peer editing can, of course, be done orally or in the form of a "quick write." However, some students find it much easier to respond when prompted by a form.

Peer Editing Response
Upper Grade

The piece I read was _____

by _____.

The best thing about this piece is _____

_____

_____.

If the writer wanted to change something, I would suggest _____

_____

_____

_____.

_____   _____
Peer Editor   *Date*

Ask your students to fill out this form (or one like it) after reading the work of another student. Younger students may respond with a symbol such as a happy face. Ask students to make only positive comments.

Writing Evaluation — Peer Editing Form

Reader's name _____   Date _____

Author's name _____

Title of piece _____

This piece of writing was _____

_____.

It made me feel _____

_____

The part I enjoyed most was _____

_____

_____.

Next time the author might want to work on _____

_____

_____.

Writing Checklist—Primary

This form can be duplicated for students to use as part of their own record keeping.

Writing Checklist
Primary

Name _____ Grade _____

Date	Writing Assignment	Edit	Revise	Comments

This form can be duplicated for students to use as part of their own record keeping.

Writing Checklist
Upper Grade

Name_____

Grade_____

Date Begun	Writing Assignment	1st Draft	Peer Edit	Revise	Self-Edit	Revise	Comments

Writing Log—All Grades

Make copies of this form for your students to keep track of their writing assignments as they are completed. Store them in portfolios for individual access and updating.

WRITING LOG

Name _____

ASSIGNMENT	DATE DRAFT 1	DATE DRAFT 2	DATE DRAFT 3	DATE FINAL DRAFT

Writing Evaluation—Elementary

Name_____ Date _____

Assignment _____

When I revised, I made these changes:

_____

_____

My piece is the right length because _____

_____

_____.

The content of this piece is _____

_____

_____.

I have checked the following:

spelling _____   punctuation _____   verb tense _____   pronoun agreement _____

I feel that my grade on this piece should be _____ because _____

_____

_____

_____.

Writing Evaluation—Advanced

Use this form to help a student keep a running evaluation of an individual assignment. You can add to or replace the points to be considered to suit your own areas of focus in writing. Readers can make comments or initial and date the appropriate squares.

Evaluation Form

Name _____ Date _____

Assignment _____

		Author	Partner	Teacher
Clarity	The reader can understand what I am trying to say.			
	My thoughts are logical.			
	I am writing to my audience.			
Conventions	I used capital letters correctly.			
	I used punctuation correctly.			
	My incorrect spelling in the early drafts has been corrected in the final draft.			
	My handwriting can be read easily.			
Writing Process	I have read and edited my work.			
	My writing partner has read and edited my work.			
	The teacher has read and edited my work.			

Teacher—Student Reading Conference

This form can be duplicated and used for keeping your conference records.

Student Conference Record for Reading

Date _____ Name _____

What is the title of the book you are reading?

_____

Who wrote it? _____

Have you read other books by this author? _____

Why did you choose this book? _____

_____

Tell me something about the story so far. _____

_____

_____

_____

What assignment do you plan in connection with this book? (Options: write a report, draw a poster, give an oral report to the class, write a letter to the author, etc.)

_____

Would you like to read another book by this same author? Why?

_____

Teacher Comments: _____

_____

_____

_____

Teacher—Student Writing Conference

This form can be duplicated and used for keeping your own conference records.

Student Conference Record for Writing

Date_____ Student's Name _____

What is the title of the piece you are working on now?

_____

What kind of piece is it? (story, poem, essay, report, etc.)

_____

What point have you reached in the writing process? (rough draft, self-editing, peer-editing, polishing)

_____

What do you plan to do next with this piece?

_____

_____

What do you like best about this piece?

_____

_____

Is there anything about this piece you would like to change?

_____

_____

Teacher Comments:

_____

_____

_____

Forms for Collecting Information

Two types of collection tools are offered in this section along with model activities demonstrating the use of each. You will want to modify these tools to suit your own lesson content.

Observable Behavior Assessments

Assessment Rubrics

Observable Behavior Assessment 1

Addition Using a Hundred's Chart

NCTM Standards met: 1, 2, 3, 6, 7, 8, 13

Materials: Laminated hundred's chart; colored chips or markers; scratch paper; Student Activity Sheet, page 50; pencils; Teacher Data Capture Sheet, page 51 (one for every two students)

Preparation: Set up group work area with the hundred's chart and colored chips or markers.

Model

The hundred's chart can be used to either discover or reinforce addition. For example:

$$22 + 34 = \underline{\qquad 56 \qquad}$$

The last number covered is 56, the sum of 22 + 34.

Place a red chip on 22.
(Chip colors are arbitrary)

Place blue chips on numbers 23, 24, 25, and 26, and green chips on 36, 46, and 56 (across forward four for the ones and down three for the tens).

Model for the students by first building and solving an addition (in column form, not sentence form). Self-correct and reinforce your solution by using the hundred's chart as outlined above. Repeat his process as many times as you feel are needed. Be sure to make a star or happy face beside each reinforced computation problem to show that it has been modeled on the hundred's chart. (It also serves to develop the strategy of eliminating tasks.)

As the students begin working on the Student Activity Sheet, ask them to first complete the hundred's chart by filling in the blank squares.

Guide students to rebuild each addition problem on their scratch paper into column form before completing computation and chart work. (This facilitates the reinforcing of the regrouping technique.)

Guide the students through completion of Student Activity Sheet. You might have students take turns, or each can work independently as you record your observations on the Teacher Data Capture Sheet.

Variations

➦ The answers to the computation problems can also be reinforced by using a calculator.

➦ Students can create their own computation problems by placing the chip on any number, writing that number down, then sliding the chip down a few rows and ahead a few numbers. The first number plus the number of rows down for the tens, and the number of spaces ahead for the ones will equal the number on which the chip lands.

Observable Behavior Assessments 1 (cont.)

Reinforcing Addition Using a Hundred's Chart

Name _____ Date_____

Take a look at this hundred's chart. It is missing a few numbers. Complete the chart before solving the problems at the bottom of the page.

1	2	3		5	6		8	9	10
11		13	14	15	16	17	18	19	
	22	23	24	25		27	28		30
31	32	33		35	36	37	38	39	40
41		43	44	45	46		48	49	50
51	52	53	54	55	56	57	58	59	60
61	62	63	64	65	66	67	68	69	70
71	72	73	74	75	76	77	78	79	80
81	82	83	84	85	86	87	88	89	90
91	92	93	94	95	96	97	98	99	100

Don't forget! Sliding down one row is the same as moving ahead ten spaces.

1. 22 + 25 = _____

2. 17 + 23 = _____

3. 12 + 21 = _____

4. 37 + 28 = _____

5. 21 + 7 = _____

6. 58 + 6 = _____

7. 27 + 14 = _____

8. 5 + 13 = _____

9. 13 + 29 = _____

10. 42 + 15 = _____

Observable Behavior Assessment 1 *(cont.)*

Use this Teacher Data Capture Sheet with the hundred's chart assessment on page 49.

Y = Yes, behavior exhibited; S = behavior somewhat exhibited; NE = behavior not exhibited

- -

_____   _____

Student Name   *Date*

	Y	**S**	**NE**	
1.	☐	☐	☐	... displayed an adequate understanding of the task at hand.
2.	☐	☐	☐	... contributed to the group discussion of activity.
3.	☐	☐	☐	... modeled correct use of the hundred's chart for activity.
4.	☐	☐	☐	... completed the computation for determining the sum.
5.	☐	☐	☐	... displayed an intuitive sense of number.
6.	☐	☐	☐	...reviewed his/her own work.

Overall, the student's performance _____ expectations *(circle choice)*.

went beyond   *met overall*   *met partial*   *met minimal*   *did not meet*

- -

_____   _____

Student Name   *Date*

	Y	**S**	**NE**	
1.	☐	☐	☐	... displayed an adequate understanding of the task at hand.
2.	☐	☐	☐	... contributed to the group discussion of activity.
3.	☐	☐	☐	... modeled correct use of the hundred's chart for the activity.
4.	☐	☐	☐	... completed the computation for determining the sum.
5.	☐	☐	☐	... displayed an intuitive sense of number.
6.	☐	☐	☐	... reviewed his/her own work.

Overall, the student's performance _____ expectations *(circle choice)*.

went beyond   *met overall*   *met partial*   *met minimal*   *did not meet*

Coin Values and Skip Counting

NCTM Standards met: 1, 2, 3, 4, 5, 6, 8, 13

Materials: real or manipulative coins; Student Activity Sheet, page 53; pencils, scratch paper; Teacher Data Capture Sheet, page 54 (one for each two students)

Preparation: Scatter coins and scratch paper on table top where group work will take place.

Model

Model the activity for the students by posing this problem: "I want to exchange my 75 cents, these three quarters, for dimes and nickels. How many different combinations can I create?" Together, predict and record how many different combinations might be constructed and record that number on scratch paper. Next, physically create sets of coins that equal 75 cents. For example, exchange the three quarters for seven dimes and a nickel. Skip count aloud to verify that the combination does equal 75 cents. Continue, "eleven nickels and two dimes; that's 5, 10, 15, 20, 25, 30, 35, 40, 45, 50, 55, one dime is ten more cents and one more dime gives us a total of 75 cents." Create and record a reasonable number of combinations. Guide students through the process of selecting a combination and tracing those coins on scratch paper. Be sure they either record the penny value within or under each coin. Have the students record inside the coin the number of pennies. Then, students can record the total amount under the string, thus illustrating skip counting. Before moving on to another combination, go back to evaluate how reasonable the original prediction of the number of combinations was.

Repeat the method above, this time using a number that will include pennies. Next, present this problem: "Melissa is going to buy an apple for 60 cents. How much change should she expect from her three quarters?" Act out the coin transaction to display the 15 cents change. Discuss how many ways the 15 cents could be delivered (a dime and a nickel, three nickels).

When you feel the students are ready, work together to complete numbers one and two of the Student Activity Sheet. Assign pairs of students to complete numbers three to seven. Encourage students to create both sets of coins with the coins for each combination before they record their responses on their data capture sheets. Record your observations on the Teacher Data Capture Sheet.

Variations

➻ Assign one pair of students to complete number three, and another pair to complete number 4 of the Student Activiy Sheet. Ask each group to present to another group the coins they chose to create the combination. The other group must spontaneously create another combination to equal the amount in question. Check to see whether the new combination is the same as the second way the presenting group combined the coins.

Observable Behavior Assessment 2 (cont.)

Skip Counting and Coin Combinations

Name _____ Date _____

1. How much does a cafeteria lunch cost at your school? _____

2. Trace a coin combination that would give you enough money to buy lunch. Do not forget to show your skip counting.

Use your coins and work with a partner to determine two sets of coin combinations that equal:

65 cents

3. _____ quarters _____

_____ dimes _____

_____ nickels _____

_____ pennies _____

98 cents

4. _____ quarters _____

_____ dimes _____

_____ nickels _____

_____ pennies _____

76 cents

5. _____ quarters _____

_____ dimes _____

_____ nickels _____

_____ pennies _____

44 cents

6. _____ quarters _____

_____ dimes _____

_____ nickels _____

_____ pennies _____

7. Is it possible to create even more than two combinations for these amounts? Explain your answer on the back of this paper.

Observable Behavior Assessment 2 (cont.)

Use this Teacher Data Capture Sheet with the coin values assessment on page 52.

Y = Yes, behavior exhibited; S = behavior somewhat exhibited; NE = behavior not exhibited

- -

_____   _____
Student Name   Date

	Y	S	NE	
1.	❏	❏	❏	...displayed an adequate understanding of the task at hand.
2.	❏	❏	❏	...contributed to group discussion of activity.
3.	❏	❏	❏	...displayed an understanding of coin values.
4.	❏	❏	❏	...displayed ability to skip count with coins.
5.	❏	❏	❏	...completed student activity with confidence.
6.	❏	❏	❏	...reviewed his/her work.

Overall, the student's performance _____ expectations (circle choice).

went beyond   _met overall_   _met partial_   _met minimal_   _did not meet_

- -

_____   _____
Student Name   Date

	Y	S	NE	
1.	❏	❏	❏	...displayed an adequate understanding of the task at hand.
2.	❏	❏	❏	...contributed to group discussion of activity.
3.	❏	❏	❏	...displayed an understanding of coin values.
4.	❏	❏	❏	...displayed ability to skip count with coins.
5.	❏	❏	❏	...completed student activity with confidence.
6.	❏	❏	❏	...reviewed his/her work.

Overall, the student's performance _____ expectations (circle choice).

went beyond   _met overall_   _met partial_   _met minimal_   _did not meet_

Observable Behavior Assessment 3

Time Measurement
NTCM Standards met: 1, 2, 3, 4, 5, 6, 7, 8, 10, 13

Materials: calculators, question cards (See "Preparation" below.); scratch paper; Student Data Capture Sheet, page 56; pencils; Teacher Data Capture Sheet, page 57 (one for every two students)

Preparation: Set up a group work area with the calculators and scratch paper. Prepare questions cards using one 3" x 5" (8 cm x 13 cm) index card each for these questions: How many days old are you? How many hours are there in a week? How many hours are there in a month? How many hours are there in a year? How many minutes are there in a week? How many minutes are there in two weeks?

Model

In this assessment, students use whatever tools are necessary to determine the answer to the question "How many minutes are there in a school day?", followed by responses to the questions on the Student Activity Sheet. Expect to spend one-half of the allotted time on warm-up activities, discussion, and group solutions to the questions raised during the warm-up. The remainder of the time should be spent with the students as they work in pairs to discuss and solve the questions on their activity sheets.

Begin with all students recording on their activity sheets the information asked for in "Area 1", letters A through F. (Inform students that they will use this data with the rest of the activity.)

Warm-up Activity: Model by asking the question, "How many minutes are there in our school day?" Think out loud using your estimation and mental math skills to determine how many minutes there are in the school day. Use scratch paper to record information, including estimates, actual computations, and useful notes. You may want to use calculators to reach your conclusions. The emphasis in using his approach is on the "thinking out loud" while "doing" the activity, and on inviting students to assist you in the exploration. Your questioning and their contributions will reveal a great deal about the students' mental math, estimation, and number sense skills. Conclude this warm-up by reviewing your steps and then by asking students if there might be another way to answer the question. Discuss other methods students might contribute.

Repeat the process as needed, using a new question card, or assign question cards to pairs of students. When ready, have students respond to the "Area 2" question of their data capture sheets. Ask one student in each pair to choose a card from the remaining face down stack of question cards. Have students record the chosen question in "Area 3" on their data capture sheets. Record your observations on the Teacher Data Capture Sheet.

Variations

- Create a classroom graph reflecting the age (in minutes or days) of each student. Have students determine whether minutes or days would be more precise if a month-by-month, week-by-week, or day-by-day graph were created.

Time Measurement Using Estimation, Mental Math, and Reasoning

Name_____ Date_____

Area 1

A) How many seconds in a minute? _____   D) How many days in a year? _____

B) How many minutes in an hour? _____   E) How many weeks in a year? _____

C) How many hours in a day? _____   F) How many months in a year? _____

Area 2

How many seconds are there in our school day?

_____

Area 3

Record the questions you choose here and solve. Use the back of your paper if you need more room.

_____

_____

_____

_____

_____

_____

_____

Observable Behavior Assessment 3 *(cont.)*

Use this Teacher Data Capture Sheet with the time measurement assessment on page 55.

Y = Yes, behavior exhibited; S = behavior somewhat exhibited; NE = behavior not exhibited

- -

_____   _____
Student Name   *Date*

    Y   S   NE

1. ❑ ❑ ❑ ...displayed an adequate understanding of the task at hand.
2. ❑ ❑ ❑ ...contributed to group discussion of activity.
3. ❑ ❑ ❑ ...displayed an understanding of coin values.
4. ❑ ❑ ❑ ...displayed ability to skip count with coins.
5. ❑ ❑ ❑ ...completed student activity sheet with confidence.
6. ❑ ❑ ❑ ...reviewed his/her work.

Overall, the student's performance _____ expectations *(circle choice)*.

went beyond   *met overall*   *met partial*   *met minimal*   *did not meet*

- -

_____   _____
Student Name   *Date*

    Y   S   NE

1. ❑ ❑ ❑ ...displayed an adequate understanding of the task at hand.
2. ❑ ❑ ❑ ...contributed to group discussion of activity.
3. ❑ ❑ ❑ ...displayed an understanding of coin values.
4. ❑ ❑ ❑ ...displayed ability to skip count with coins.
5. ❑ ❑ ❑ ...completed student activity sheet with confidence.
6. ❑ ❑ ❑ ...reviewed his/her work.

Overall, the student's performance _____ expectations *(circle choice)*.

went beyond   *met overall*   *met partial*   *met minimal*   *did not meet*

This generalized task rubric can be customized as necessary to fit a particular situation, as on pages 59-61, or used generically, as presented on page 62.

Generalized Task Rubric

6 (Narrative description of a performance that would be considered exemplary.)

5 **(Narrative description of an acceptable performance.)**

4 (Narrative description of a performance that is not quite as good as "5" but is clearly an acceptable paper.)

3 (Narrative description of a performance that is a little better than "2".)

2 **(Narrative description of an unacceptable performance in concept goals, but effort was made to complete task.)**

1 (Narrative description of a performance that is not acceptable. Student made little effort to participate.)

0 (No effort was made to participate.)

This completed generalized task rubric could be used to assess performance for Student Activity A on page 61.

Generalized Task Rubric

6   Student completed task; shared not only "problems built" but his or her strategy for determining solutions. Demonstrated very good use of mental math and firm understanding of "a remainder" at the symbolic level. Strong understanding of inverse nature of division and multiplication. Good use of language and could explain process, model odd/even numbers.

5   Student completed task for various sums fitting into the range and exhibited the use of a strategy but was limited in his or her use of descriptive language. No hesitation to offer more than one solution. Good mental math for determining number combinations. Basic understanding of the inverse nature of division and multiplication.

4   Student hesitated but could use language to define odd, even, quotient, and remainder at the symbolic level. Student too consumed in procedure and with finding only one solution.

3   Student displayed a basic understanding of what was being requested but did not know where to begin solving the problem. By observing others and asking questions, he/she did eventually offer input the solutions.

2   Student displayed knowledge of number only at the concrete level. No comfort level displayed with the terms required, or a "remainder", even at the concrete level. He/she relied almost completely on the group to provide "correct answers."

1   Student sat with group, but only observed.

0   Student chose not to participate in group or activity.

This complete generalized task rubric could be used to assess performance for Student Activity B on page 61.

Generalized Task Rubric

6 Student displayed outstanding understanding of a fraction and of the symbolic fraction structure. He/she could explain both confidently. Displayed firm grasp of common denominators and math facts. Understood this to be an inappropriate opportunity to use the calculator and relied primarily on mental math. Displayed at least three solutions.

5 Student able to define and display terms such as denominator, numerator, and digit. Understood use of the digit cards to help with elimination and guess and check. Offered at least two solutions. Good use of paper and pencil as recording device.

4 Student displayed adequate understanding of fraction; stronger concretely than symbolically. Comfortably used manipulatives, (fraction pieces), and digit cards to build solutions. Used language appropriately when asked. Hesitated to use scratch paper to take notes even though doing so was encouraged.

3 Student displayed basic understanding of fractions, but only at the concrete level. He/she could build a model using manipulatives and with guidance, transfer the information to symbolic form. Elicited language was scattered and missing mathematical terms.

2 Displayed great confusion about the inverse relationship between denominator and size of fractional pieces. Relied totally on manipulatives to see a contributed solution. Could discuss the concrete form, but could not transfer concrete to symbolic to complete problem.

1 Student sat with group, but only observed.

0 Student chose not to participate in group or activity.

Assessment Rubrics *(cont.)*

Assessment A

Division with a remainder: ones dividing tens

Complete the problem to reflect a two-digit even number quotient and an odd number remainder.

You may use a digit more than once.

Assessment B

Addition of fractions: combinations to 1

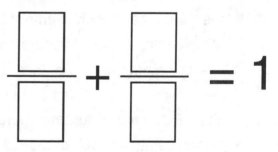

Choose four digit cards from

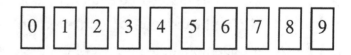

to form a problem with the sum of 1.

You may use a digit more than once.

This completed generalized task rubric could be used in its most generic form.

Generalized Task Rubric

6 Exemplary Achievement

- Demonstrates full understanding of major concepts
  - — uses language to describe process or strategy
  - — uses tools including paper and pencil, calculator, and mental math very effectively and when appropriate
  - — reflects and generalizes about process and purpose

5 Commendable Achievement

- Demonstrates detailed understanding of major concepts
  - — uses language, to a point, to describe process or strategy
  - — uses tools, including paper and pencil, calculator, and mental math effectively
  - — reflects and generalizes about process and purpose

4 Adequate Achievement

- Demonstrates a fundamental level of understanding the major concepts
  - — uses language at the literal level
  - — uses tools, including paper and pencil, calculator, and mental math, but depends too much on the calculator when mental math or pencil and paper would serve more effectively

3 Some Evidence of Achievement

- Demonstrates partial understanding of the major concepts
  - — is stronger at "doing" than at describing with language
  - — solves basic problems at the concrete level only

2 Limited Evidence of Achievement

- Demonstrates a lack of required skills to complete task
  - — attempts task but does not recognize "incorrect" solutions
  - — hesitates to discuss any aspect of situation

1 Minimal Evidence of Achievement

- Demonstrates a lack of understanding of task
  - — Can combine objects to create a set, but makes no connection to symbols or generalized process

0 No participation or response

©1995 Teacher Created Materials, Inc.

Use this blank model to develop your own generalized task rubric. Begin by completing the criteria for levels 5 and 2.

Generalized Task Rubric

6

5

4

3

2

1

0

Forms for Collecting Information

It is easy to collect information about science for your portfolios by documenting an investigation performed by your students. The pages that follow consist of a simple investigation, a variety of response sheets, and a teacher's checklist. Additional information is included about creating a rubric to document the checklist.

You can try this investigation for practice and then adapt the forms to suit your own investigations and create your own checklists and rubrics.

An Investigation of Textures

Textures: An Investigation

Relevant Skills

Observing/Collecting Data/Using Tools/Classifying/Inferring/Communicating in Writing

Knowledge Base

- Has knowledge of senses

- Has vocabulary for textures

Setting Up the Investigation

- Gather together a large assortment of things representing different textures: fabric, sandpaper, wood scraps, fur, feather, marbles, and so on. Either provide these things in quantities of small samples or provide scissors for cutting off pieces.

- Tell students that they will be investigating the textures of things (how things feel).

- Have a large-group brainstorming session to review the senses of touch and to think of words that describe textures. (Suggestions: smooth, rough, hard, soft, grainy, fluffy, bumpy, slippery, sticky, scratchy, sharp, pitted, creamy.) Write the words on the chalkboard and later transfer them to poster board for long-term classroom display during this investigation.

- Give students "Response Sheet 1: Observing/Collecting Data." Have each student study the classroom samples, feel them, and choose samples to observe further. They will mount six of their favorite samples on "Response Sheet 1." If they choose things that cannot be glued on, they can staple together paper to make small pouches of paper that can contain the samples. Have students glue the pouches to the response sheet.

- Have students work in groups to complete "Response Sheet 2: Observing/Using Tools." They will also need their completed "Response Sheet 1" for this activity.

- Have students list as many things as they can under each of the texture words on "Response Sheet 3: Classifying." You may have each student generate the texture words or you can write the words you choose on the sheet before duplicating.

- Have students complete "Response Sheet 4: Inferring." They can then meet in groups to discuss their conclusions. Did they all reach similar conclusions? Did anyone discover something different? How can they check conclusions?

- Use "Response Sheet 5: Communicating in Writing" to prompt each student to write a paragraph about textures. (Currently there is some difference of opinion about mixing science and writing skills, so you will need to decide whether this fits into your own philosophy of teaching science. You can easily omit this part of the investigation.)

- Have students complete the Investigation Overview (page 72).

- Complete the teacher's checklist on page 73.

Textures: Response Sheet 1

Observing/Collecting Data

Name_____ Date_____

In the boxes below, mount your six favorite texture samples.

Label them with one or more words that describe their textures.

_____	_____
_____	_____
_____	_____

Textures: Response Sheet 2

Observing/Using Tools

Name_____ Date_____

In the boxes below, write the names of the samples you mounted on Response Sheet 1. Look again at the samples you mounted on Response Sheet 1 using a magnifier. Think of a word that tells how each one looks. Write that word under the box on this sheet.

The sample I mounted in this box was

_____.

It looks _____.

The sample I mounted in this box was

_____.

It looks _____.

The sample I mounted in this box was

_____.

It looks _____.

The sample I mounted in this box was

_____.

It looks _____.

The sample I mounted in this box was

_____.

It looks _____.

The sample I mounted in this box was

_____.

It looks _____.

Classifying

Name_____ Date_____

On the lines below, you will find texture words. (If they are not already there, your teacher may ask you to think up and write in your own.) Under each texture word, write examples of things with that texture. For example, under Slippery you could write "ice" and "oil."

Texture: Response Sheet 4

Inferring

Name_____ Date _____

Think about what you have discovered so far about textures. Complete the sentences below.

1. Things that **look** bumpy will probably **feel**

_____

_____.

2. Things that **look** shiny will probably **feel**

_____

_____.

3. Things that **look** pointed will probably **feel**

_____

_____.

4. Things that **look** fluffy will probably **feel**

_____

_____.

5. Things that **look** slow when you pour them will probably **feel**

_____

_____.

Texture: Response Sheet 5

Communicating in Writing

Name _____ Date _____

Writing Situation

You have learned a lot about using your senses to discover how things feel to the touch. Someone from another class has asked you to explain what you have learned.

Directions for Writing

Write a paragraph telling something you have discovered about texture. Try to explain it so someone from another class will understand it too. Use capitals and periods to begin and end your sentences. If you do not know how to spell a word, write it the way it sounds.

_____

_____

_____

_____

_____

_____

_____

_____

_____

_____

_____

_____

_____

_____

_____

Rubric for Science Paragraph

Score 3: High Pass

Student

... responds to prompt; explains something about texture.

... writes several sentences using capitals and ending punctuation.

... uses spelling (both real and invented/phonetic) that does not inhibit reader's understanding.

Score 2: Pass

Student

... responds to prompt; tells something about texture.

... expresses complete thoughts although sentences may be fragmented or run ons.

... uses spelling (both real and invented/phonetic) that, for the most part, does not inhibit the reader's understanding.

Score 1: Needs Revision

Student

... may not respond to prompt.

... expresses self in ways that inhibits reader's understanding.

... does not demonstrate understanding of sound/symbol relationships or of word boundaries.

Score 0: No Response

Investigation Overview

Name_____ Date _____

Answer these questions about your investigation of textures.

1. Which six samples did you choose?

_____

_____

_____

2. Did looking at your samples through a magnifier help you to do your investigation? How?

_____

_____

_____

3. Name something that feels slippery.

_____

_____

_____

4. Something that feels rough usually looks...

_____

_____

_____

5. What did you tell about in the paragraph you wrote?

_____

_____

_____

Textures: Teacher's Checklist

Reproduce this form for each student in your class. *Rate the appropriate sections on this list as you collect the response forms. Stack each student's forms with the checklist on top and place them in the portfolios.*

TEXTURES: INVESTIGATION	Observing	Collecting Data	Using Tools	Classifying	Inferring	Communicating Writing
Name_____ Date_____						
Make a quick assessment of quality from 5 to 1 (5 is high).						
Response 1 Observing/Collecting Data						
Response 2 Observing/Using Tools						
Response 3 Classifying						
Response 4 Inferring						
Response 5 Communicating in Writing						
Response 6 Investigation Overview						

Observations are usually documented with anecdotal records and checklists of one kind or another. They are collected in portfolios and are compared with each other as a reflection of growth over a period of time.

If a teacher wants a more specific criterion for quality than is provided by most checklists, he or she can create a rubric to build in a scale of achievement. The checklist that accompanies the investigation of texture contains this direction: "Make a quick assessment of quality from 5 to 1 (5 is high)." One could add a definition of each number of these checklists if desired. For example, the definitions below would define gradations in quality for "Textures."

5 =	understands that texture is related to sense of touch; uses touch to differentiate among textures; relates how things look to how they feel; chooses and uses scientific tools to assist observations; can group by criteria; generalizes; has wide and accurate vocabulary to communicate observations which may be different and original
4 =	knows that texture is related to sense of touch; uses touch to differentiate among textures; see a relationship between how some things look and how they feel; uses scientific tools to assist observations; can group by criteria; generalizes; has wide vocabulary to communicate observations
3 =	is aware that texture is related to sense of touch; uses touch to differentiate between opposite textures (rough/smooth); recognizes a relationship between how something looks and how it feels when it is pointed out; may or may not use scientific tools to assist observations; can group by one criterion only; needs help in making generalizations; has adequate vocabulary to communicate observations
2 =	may not be aware that texture is related to sense of touch; does not always see the difference between textures; may or may not recognize a relationship between how something looks and how it feels when it is pointed out; makes no attempt to use scientific tools to assist observations; cannot classify; needs help in making generalizations; does not have adequate vocabulary to communicate observation
1 =	is not aware that texture is related to sense of touch; makes no attempt to participate in investigation or tries to participate with little or no success

These gradations in quality are the things a teacher sees without consciously noting each one. The benefit of having these gradations listed is being able to communicate them —to the administration, to other teachers who want to try the same kind of teaching and assessment, and to parents at report card time.

Social Studies

Forms for Collecting Information

Concept Development Checklist

Student's Name _____ Grade _____

Rating Scale: 1 = Rarely Observed
2 = Occasionally Observed
3 = Often Observed

Concept				
History	**1**	**2**	**3**	**4**
Understands reasons for studying history				
Understands time lines/chronology				
Has a sense of empathy for the past				
Has an appreciation for our multicultural society				
Understands principles of democracy				
Appreciates country's ideals				
Understands origins of important historical documents				
Recognizes importance of religion in human society				
Is familiar with basic ideas of religion				
Understands conflict resolution				
Understands the role of laws				
Understands different political systems				
Geography	**1**	**2**	**3**	**4**
Uses locational skills				
Understands awareness of place				
Understands world regions				
Identifies and uses map and globe symbols				
Understands locational terms				
Understands directional terms				
Constructs maps				

Concept Development Checklist *(cont.)*

Concept				
Citizenship	1	2	3	4
Understands duties of our leaders				
Understands voting procedures				
Has respect for human rights				
Understands responsibility of being a citizen in a democratic society				
Shows commitment to democratic values				
Critical Thinking Skills	1	2	3	4
Identifies central issues/problems				
Determines relevant information				
Distinguishes fact, opinion, and reasoned judgment				
Recognizes stereotypes, bias, and propaganda				
Analyzes cause/effect relationships				
Tests conclusions/hypotheses				
Justifies conclusions				
Identifies reasonable alternatives				
Predicts consequences of events				
Participation Skills	1	2	3	4
Expresses personal convictions				
Listens to differing points of view				
Formulates appropriate questions				
Recognizes personal bias				
Demonstrates skills of:				
persuasion				
compromise				
debate				
negotiation				

Concept Development Checklist (cont.)

Concept				
Study Skills	**1**	**2**	**3**	**4**
Locates information				
Selects appropriate information				
Organizes information				
Acquires information by:				
listening				
observing				
locating community resources				
reading literature				
referring to primary sources				
Reads and interprets:				
maps				
globes				
models				
diagrams				
graphs				
charts				
time lines				
political cartoons				
Other	**1**	**2**	**3**	**4**

Interest Inventory

Name _____ Date_____

1. What is your favorite subject in school? _____

2. What is your least favorite subject in school? _____

3. What do you like to do in your free time? _____

   _____

4. Who is your best friend? _____

5. What is your favorite sport? _____

6. What is your favorite animal? _____

7. Name something you do very well. _____

   _____

8. Name something that makes you angry. _____

   _____

9. What is your favorite T.V. show? _____

10. What is your favorite book? _____

11. What is your favorite movie? _____

12. If you could meet a famous person, who would it be?_____

13. Why would you like to meet that person? _____

   _____

14. What would you like to be when you grow up? _____

   _____

15. What would you like to learn in school this year? _____

   _____

   _____

Social Studies Survey

Name _____	Date _____

1. How do you feel about studying social studies? _____

   _____

   _____

2. Is it important to know about the past? Why?_____

   _____

3. Is it important to know about other people and cultures? Why?_____

   _____

4. What do you enjoy about the study of history? _____

   _____

   _____

5. What do you find frustrating about the study of history? _____

   _____

   _____

6. What would you like to learn about in Social Studies this year? _____

   _____

   _____

   _____

Monthly Reading Log

Use this form to record all the reading you do in one month.

Name _____

Month _____

Title of Book	Author	Historical Topic	Pages	Comments

What was your favorite book of the month? _____

_____

What was the best part of the book? _____

_____

What do you plan to read next month? _____

_____

Book Review Form

Name _____

Title of book _____

Author _____

Number of pages _____

Historical topic _____

1. Why did you choose this book? _____

_____

_____

2. Summarize the story._____

_____

_____

_____

3. How do you rate this book?
    _____ Exciting
    _____ Interesting
    _____ O.K.
    _____ Dull

4. Why did you give the book that rating? _____

_____

5. Was the book historically accurate? Give examples. _____

_____

_____

_____

_____

Reviewer's signature _____

Literature Response Guide

Name_____ Date_____

Use this guide to assist you in literature response journal writing.

Step One

Summary:
Summarize the story in your own words, including details on characters, main events, setting, historical period, climax, and resolution.

Step Two

Your Reactions:
1. How did the main character feel when faced with a conflict?

2. Why did the character react the way he or she did?

3. Should the character have acted that way?

4. What would you have done?

5. What does the story remind you of?

6. What did you like about the book?

7. What did you dislike about the book?

8. If you were the writer, what would you change?

9. Did the author make you feel that you were transported to that time in history?

Facts and Feelings Chart

Name _____

Unit of Study _____

Historical Novel _____

Historical Facts	Character Feelings/Reactions

84
©1995 Teacher Created Materials, Inc.

Performance Task

Types and Descriptions

Comparison Task: The student is required to compare two or more people, places, or things.

Classification Task: The student is asked to classify, or put into categories, certain people, places, or things.

Position Support Task: The student is asked to take a position on a subject or issue and defend that position.

Application Task: The student is asked to apply his or her knowledge in a new situation.

Analyzing Perspectives Task: The student is asked to analyze two to three different perspectives and then choose the perspective he or she supports.

Decision Making Task: The student must identify the factors that caused a certain decision to be made.

Historical Perspective Task: The student must consider differing theories to answer basic historical questions.

Predictive Task: The student must make predictions about what could have happened or will happen in the future.

Problem Solving Task: The student must create a solution to a specific problem.

Experimental Task: The student sets up an experiment to test a hypothesis.

Invention Task: The student must create something new and unique.

Error Identification Task: The student must identify specific errors.

Performance Task Recording Sheet

Task

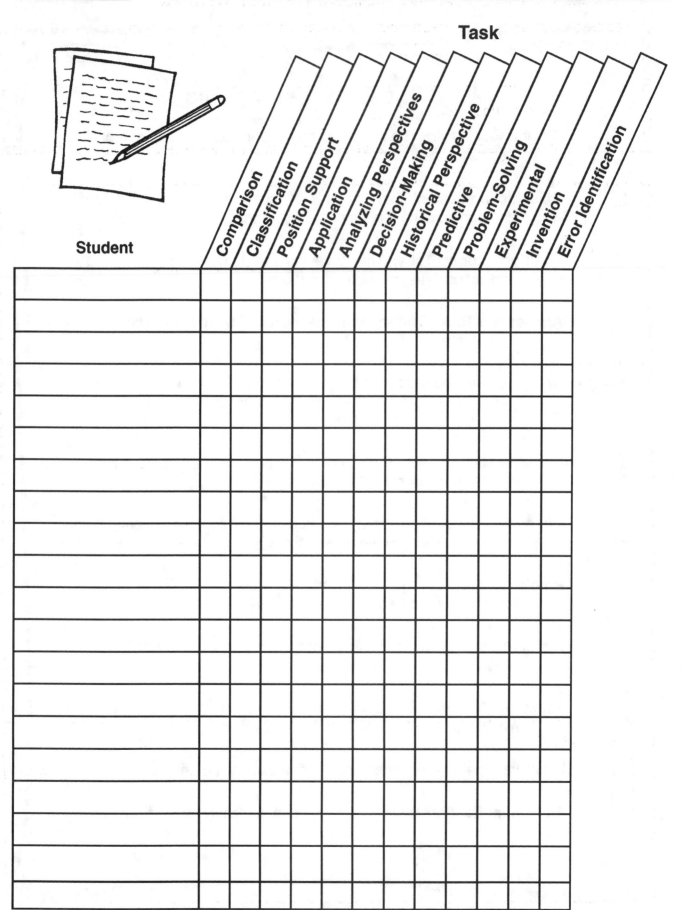

Student	Comparison	Classification	Position Support	Application	Analyzing Perspectives	Decision-Making	Historical Perspective	Predictive	Problem-Solving	Experimental	Invention	Error Identification

86

©1995 Teacher Created Materials, Inc.

Performance Task Recording Sheet *(cont.)*

Student's Name _____

Date _____ Grade Level _____

Type of Performance Task _____

Description of Task:

Strengths:

Weaknesses:

Assist student with:

Group Process Evaluation

Name _____

Group Members _____

Cooperative Task _____

_____

1. Describe the effectiveness of your group on the task. _____

   _____

   _____

   _____

2. What were the group's strengths? _____

   _____

   _____

   _____

   _____

3. What frustrations did the group encounter? _____

   _____

   _____

   _____

   _____

4. Did all members of the group participate? _____

5. Did you listen to each other? _____

6. Name two ways in which your group could improve in order to be more effective on your next cooperative task.

   a. _____

   _____

   b. _____

   _____

88 *©1995 Teacher Created Materials, Inc.*

Peer Evaluation Form

Cooperative Groups

Name _____

Group Members _____

Cooperative Task _____

_____

Role	Effective	Ineffective	Comments
Reader			
Recorder			
Manager			
Leader			
Monitor			

Teacher Evaluation Form

Cooperative Groups

Cooperative task _____

Date_____

Number of students in the group _____

Members of the group _____

_____

1. How were decisions made? _____

_____

_____

2. How did students help each other achieve a common goal? _____

_____

_____

3. Did you have to intervene at any time? If so, why? _____

_____

_____

4. Did the group meet the cooperative investigation objective? _____

   Evidence or examples: _____

_____

_____

_____

_____

Comments on individual group members:

_____

_____

_____

_____

Independent Research Contract

Contents

Name_____ Date _____

The Project

My research topic is _____

What do I need to know? _____

_____

_____

_____

Where will I get this information? _____

_____

_____

_____

The Time Line

I will begin my research on _____.

I will present a progress report on_____.

I will conclude my study on _____.

I will present my final report on _____.

The Presentation

_____ I will present my research in a paper.

_____ I will do an oral presentation of my research to the class.

_____ I will make a project (display, diorama, video, etc.) to present my research.

Research Project Evaluation

Name _____

Research Project _____

(1 = poor, 2 = average, 3 = good, 4 = excellent)

Skill	Score			
	1	**2**	**3**	**4**
Information obtained from several sources Examples:				
Project meets requirements Examples:				
Extras included (cover, pictures) Examples:				
Oral report given to class Examples:				
Extra-credit work Examples:				

92
©1995 Teacher Created Materials, Inc.

Additional Forms

Collecting Information in Other Areas

The types of information that reflect a student's interest or ability in areas that are usually thought of as "artistic" are most conveniently obtained through observation. Various checklists can be used for this purpose. Checklists for the visual arts, music, and movement are included in this section.

Checklists

Visual Arts

Check those qualities/behaviors that apply to the activity or project.

Name _____ Date _____

Activity/Project _____

1. Accurately perceives objects

_____ ♦ describes shapes

_____ ♦ describes colors

_____ ♦ describes textures

_____ ♦ describes sizes

_____ ♦ compares attributes of various objects

2. Uses imagination to move objects through space

_____ ♦ identifies or describes object rotated

_____ ♦ identifies or describes object from another perspective

3. Creates a concrete representation of his or her perceptions

_____ ♦ two-dimensional form

_____ ♦ three-dimensional form

4. Understands and uses graphic organizers

_____ ♦ mapping

_____ ♦ clustering

_____ ♦ doodling

_____ ♦ color coding

Use of Visual Materials

Check those qualities/behaviors that apply to the activity or project.

Name _____ Date _____

Activity/Project _____

1. Can gather information from visuals

_____ ♦ posters

_____ ♦ bulletin boards

_____ ♦ displays

_____ ♦ videos

_____ ♦ slides

_____ ♦ overhead transparencies

2. Uses visual-spatial creations to express comprehension

_____ ♦ sketches

_____ ♦ models

_____ ♦ mind maps

_____ ♦ time lines

3. Uses the computer

_____ ♦ computer graphics

_____ ♦ interactive computer activities

Response to Music

Check those qualities/behaviors that apply to the activity or project.

Name _____ Date _____

Activity/Project_____

1. Responds to pitch in music

_____ ♦ reproduces a melody vocally

_____ ♦ sings a scale

_____ ♦ jumps an octave vocally

_____ ♦ identifies a tone that is off key in a familiar melody

2. Responds to rhythm in music

_____ ♦ reproduces a beat

_____ ♦ moves in response to different rhythms

3. Responds to mood of a musical selection

_____ ♦ identifies music as happy (major) or sad (minor)

_____ ♦ identifies music as energizing or relaxing

4. Identifies types of music

_____ ♦ classical

_____ ♦ rock

_____ ♦ jazz

Use of Musical/Rhythmic Materials

Check those qualities/behaviors that apply to the activity or project.

Name _____ Date_____

Activity/Project_____

1. Uses musical selections

_____ ♦ represents or illustrates a period in history

_____ ♦ represents or illustrates a piece of literature

_____ ♦ represents or illustrates a piece of visual art

2. Creates a melody

_____ ♦ expresses a concept

_____ ♦ expresses a mood

_____ ♦ intensifies a learning experience

3. Uses rhythm

_____ ♦ participates in choral reading

_____ ♦ practices a math or language concept (times table, spelling)

4. Creates a rhythm

_____ ♦ makes up a chant

_____ ♦ makes up a rap song

_____ ♦ makes up new words to a popular song to illustrate aconcept

Movement

Check those qualities/behaviors that apply to the kinesthetic activity or project.

Name _____ Date _____

Activity/Project _____

Social

_____ ♦ understands body language

_____ ♦ "reads" postures and gestures of others

_____ ♦ can establish own personal space

_____ ♦ respects personal space of others

_____ ♦ changes appropriate personal space based on relationships

_____ ♦ knows how to emphasize a point with gestures

Academic

_____ ♦ learns how to do something by watching and imitating

_____ ♦ uses manipulatives to explore and explain ideas

_____ ♦ learns from hands-on activities and experiments

_____ ♦ enjoys cut and paste activities

_____ ♦ makes three-dimensional models to assist or demonstrate
learning

_____ ♦ participates in role-playing

_____ ♦ uses eye-hand coordination

©1995 Teacher Created Materials, Inc.

Movement *(cont.)*

Check those qualities/behaviors that apply to the kinesthetic activity or project.

Name _____ Date _____

Activity/Project _____

Expressive

_____ ♦ communicates through movement

_____ ♦ imitates demonstrated body postures and movements

_____ ♦ uses dance to communicate mood and ideas

_____ ♦ conveys meaning with the use of mime

_____ ♦ participates in creative drama

Athletic

_____ ♦ uses movement to release tension and/or emotion

_____ ♦ uses movement to increase intake of oxygen for energy

_____ ♦ demonstrates coordination and physical fitness

_____ ♦ enjoys playing physical games

_____ ♦ learns games/sports easily

_____ ♦ participates in sports

_____ ♦ excels at one or more sports

The Paper Avalanche

As you have probably deduced after browsing through the various forms in the preceding section, portfolio assessment depends on paper—lots of paper. You cannot let it get ahead of you for even a day. The suggestions on page 141 will help you avoid being buried alive in paper, but for now, think about how you will set up your filing system.

Filing the First Paper

Pretend for a moment that you have made the containers for your Collection Portfolios and decided on the samples you will collect and the forms you will use. The next step is to visualize this scenario in your classroom: It is the first day of school and the students have just completed a quick-write that you want to save. How do you get those papers into the correct portfolios without creating a mob scene that will destroy your whole system of classroom management (or without staying after school and doing it yourself)? Actually, after checking on a few basic skills with your students, you have a couple of options.

Basic Skills

Students should know and recognize their names written with the last name first.

Students should know how to file things by grasping the correct folder.

It will help if students know how to use the alphabet to put things in order and find things. This is not absolutely essential for filing. Younger children may look through all the folders until they find the right one. However, it is much faster to use the alphabet, and even very young students will learn to refer to the letters you have posted in the room if they are not sure of how to do this.

Options

You can have each student file his her own paper. A good way to do this is to post a chart with a list of your students' names on it near your portfolios. Jot down the name of the sample to be filed at the top of one vertical column and ask students to place a check in the appropriate box when they put that paper into their portfolios.

You can have one or more Portfolio Aides who do all your filing. They can help each other, take turns, or split the job any number of ways. The job can be routed through the whole class or stay with the students who need the extra responsibility.

You can combine these two options by having students file their own papers and by having aides check the files occasionally for misfiled papers.

Class List for Filing Portfolio Papers

Write the name of the assignment at the top of a column so students can check it off as they file their papers. Filing aides can also use this form to be sure each student handed in a paper to be filed.

Names	Assignments				

Portfolio Aide Schedule

Use this schedule or one like it to schedule your Portfolio Aides.

DATES		NAMES	

Step Four of the Portfolio Planner

When to Sort

You can decide to sort through the Collection Portfolios at any time that is convenient and/or meaningful to you and your students. You might decide to do this once a month, at the end of a thematic unit, before report card conferences, or whenever the Collection Portfolios get too full to manage.

What to Sort

Sorting the papers in the Collection Portfolio is the most meaningful part of portfolio assessment—the students actually begin to take control of their own learning process as they see and reflect on the progress that has been made and then participate in deciding what to save in a Showcase Portfolio. Sorting the papers is also a practical process—the best or most meaningful samples will stay, but the rest of the papers will go home!

How to Sort

Sorting is a time-consuming process, but it is a real part of the instructional program. It does not go home with the teacher. It happens right in class. It can go like this:

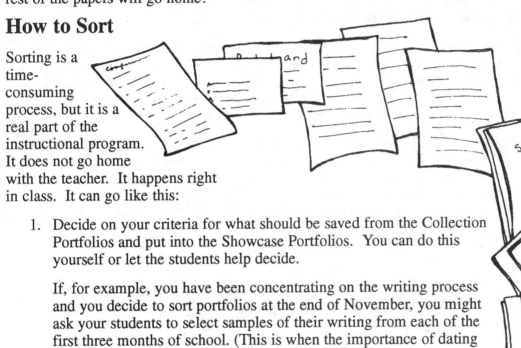

1. Decide on your criteria for what should be saved from the Collection Portfolios and put into the Showcase Portfolios. You can do this yourself or let the students help decide.

   If, for example, you have been concentrating on the writing process and you decide to sort portfolios at the end of November, you might ask your students to select samples of their writing from each of the first three months of school. (This is when the importance of dating papers becomes very clear!)

   If you have been doing thematic teaching and have completed two themes, you might want the students to separate the two themes and then select samples from each theme: a reading checklist, a piece of writing, a related math paper, a social studies report, a science investigation, and a reflection paper.

   No matter how structured your list of criteria, allow room for work that is meaningful to the student. You can have the student clearly label a paper you would be happy to omit from the Showcase Portfolio as "My Favorite Story" or "Work I Want to Keep" if its inclusion really offends your sense of what is relevant and important.

   A list of forms and suggestions to help you with your criteria statement are included on page 105.

How to Sort *(cont.)*

2. Pass out the portfolios and have the students take out the papers and arrange them chronologically as they browse through their work. (Dates!) Call their attention to the progress they have made. Let them enjoy themselves and talk to both you and their peers about what they discover. Most students are shocked to see the changes in the quality of their work over a given period of time.

3. Pass out and discuss your list of criteria (or discuss your criteria as you write your list on the board) and have the students make their choices. These papers should be set to one side for the Showcase Portfolios, and everything that was not selected should be bundled up to take home. With small children, you may want to put a rubber band around the work and present it to the student(s) at conference time with an explanation of how the work was sorted. Even though you will be showing them the best work and the evidence of progress made in their students' Showcase Portfolio, some parents are more impressed by quantity.

Ask students to pull out your anecdotal records while they are making their choices. If you color-coded your papers, you can simply ask them to make a stack of the blue (or whatever) papers for you. While this is going on, walk around the room with a stapler and pick up and staple together each student's stack of anecdotal records. Stick them back into the now-empty Collection Portfolios or save them for your Portfolio Aide(s) to file later.

4. Have students reflect on the progress they can see in their work. This is a slightly different process from reflecting on a single product, so discuss the idea of seeing progress made over a period of time. This reflection on progress should be included with the papers chosen for the Showcase Portfolio. (Forms for this special kind of reflection, together with a lesson plan, a teacher script, and a student prompt for a reflective essay, are provided on pages 117–122.)

5. Put the old Collection Portfolios away in their accessible place and get ready to start the Showcase Portfolio!

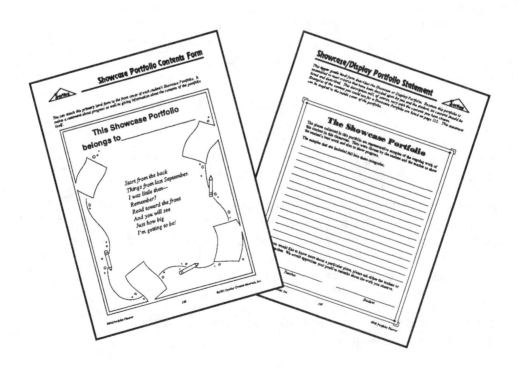

Listing Criteria/Reflecting on Progress

Forms and Suggestions

The forms, lists, and suggestions that follow appear in different styles and for different grade levels. Browse through them to find the ones that are appropriate for you or adapt them to suit your own purposes.

You can attach this **primary level** form to the front cover of each student's Showcase Portfolio. It makes a statement about progress as well as giving information about the contents of the portfolio itself.

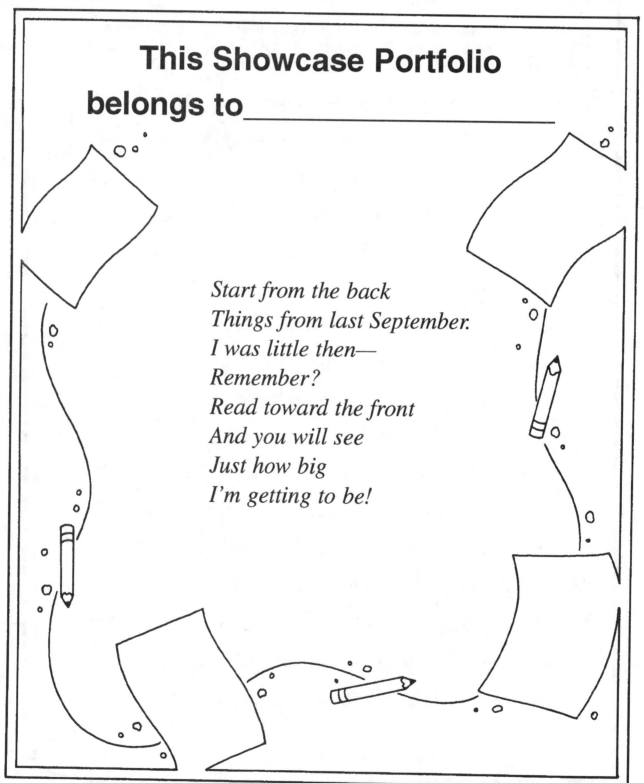

This Showcase Portfolio
belongs to _____

Start from the back
Things from last September.
I was little then—
Remember?
Read toward the front
And you will see
Just how big
I'm getting to be!

©1995 Teacher Created Materials, Inc.

Showcase/Display Portfolio Statement

*This **upper grade level** form describes the Showcase or Display Portfolio. Because this portfolio is assembled to meet criteria that have been decided upon by you and the student, its contents should be listed and described. This description will, of course, vary with the contents you have chosen. Examples of the content you could use for a Showcase Portfolio are listed on page 115. This statement can be stapled to the inside cover of the portfolio.*

The Showcase Portfolio

The pieces collected in this portfolio are representative samples of the ongoing work of this student in this classroom. They were chosen by the student and the teacher to show the student's best work and also to show progress.

The samples that are included fall into these categories:

_____

_____

_____

_____

_____

_____

_____

_____

_____

_____

_____

_____

_____

_____

If you would like to know more about a particular piece, please ask either the student or the teacher. We would appreciate your positive remarks about the work you observe.

_____   _____
Teacher   *Student*

Showcase Portfolio Contents Sheet

*You can attach a copy of this **advanced level** form to the front cover of each student's Showcase Portfolio. It makes a statement about the criteria used in choosing the work as well as giving information about the contents.*

This Showcase Portfolio is the property of

_____

It contains the following samples of my work:

_____

_____

_____

_____

_____

_____

_____

_____

_____

_____

_____

_____

_____

These samples were chosen to show:

_____

_____

_____

_____

_____

_____

_____

Primary Writing Process Contents Form

Reproduce this form and staple it on top of a writing process packet. Check off the relevant items and add the packet to the portfolio.

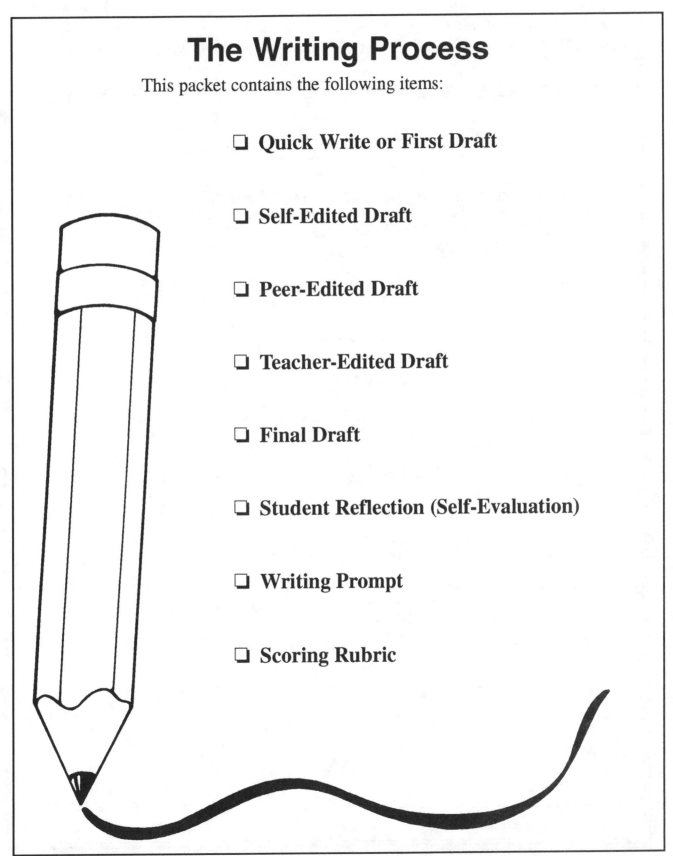

The Writing Process

This packet contains the following items:

❏ **Quick Write or First Draft**

❏ **Self-Edited Draft**

❏ **Peer-Edited Draft**

❏ **Teacher-Edited Draft**

❏ **Final Draft**

❏ **Student Reflection (Self-Evaluation)**

❏ **Writing Prompt**

❏ **Scoring Rubric**

The statement that appears below includes a description of the writing process. It will clarify the inclusion in a portfolio of pieces in various stages of completion. It can be stapled to the inside front cover of a portfolio devoted to language arts or placed at the front of the writing section of a more general portfolio.

The Writing Process

The pieces of writing in this portfolio reflect the different stages in the writing process. Some are quick writes. Some are edited and revised first or second drafts. Some are completed or polished pieces that have been through the entire writing process:

- exposure to background information

- brainstorming

- first draft

- peer editing

- self-editing

- revision

- rewriting

We hope you will be as interested in the process as in the pieces that are obviously finished.

_____   _____
Teacher   Student

Advanced Writing Process Statement

Reproduce this form and staple it on top of a writing process packet. Check off the relevant items and add the packet to the portfolio.

The Writing Process

This packet contains the following items:

❑ **Quick Write or First Draft**

❑ **Self-Edited Draft**

❑ **Peer-Edited Draft**

❑ **Teacher-Edited Draft**

❑ **Final Draft**

❑ **Student Reflection (Self-Evaluation)**

❑ **Writing Prompt**

❑ **Scoring Rubric**

*Reproduce this **primary level** form and attach it to the work that represents a thematic unit you have included in the portfolio. If the whole portfolio is devoted to one theme, attach this form to the inside or outside of the cover. List the items you have chosen to save.*

Our Thematic Unit on

_____

This packet contains the following items:

❑ **Reading**

❑ **Writing**

❑ **Social Studies**

❑ **Science**

❑ **Art**

❑ **Music**

❑ **Other**

❑ **Student Reflections on Work**

Thematic Unit Contents Form

This **upper grade level** *form is designed to be used in the self-contained classroom or by the single-subject teacher who is attempting to make connections across the curriculum. Make a copy of the form and attach it to the work that represents a thematic unit you have asked students to include in their portfolios. If the whole portfolio is devoted to one theme, attach this form to the inside or outside of the cover.*

This thematic unit on_____is the property of

_____.

This packet contains the following items:

Reading: _____

_____

Writing:_____

_____

Social Studies:_____

_____

Science: _____

_____

Art: _____

_____

Other: _____

_____

Student Reflections on Work: _____

_____

_____

Interdisciplinary Unit Contents

*This **advanced level** form is designed to be used for a unit taught by an interdisciplinary team. Make a copy and attach it to the work that you have asked students to include in their portfolios to reflect that unit. If the whole portfolio is devoted to one unit, attach this form to the inside or outside of the cover.*

This unit on _____ is the property of

_____.

It is the outcome of work in these areas:

_____   _____

_____   _____
            Course   Teacher

_____   _____
            Course   Teacher

_____   _____
            Course   Teacher

            Course   Teacher

It contains the following items:

_____

_____

_____

_____

_____

_____

_____

_____

Examples of Showcase Content

Sample #1

2	Quick Writes
2	Journal Entries
1	Complete Writing Process Package
1	Peer Editing Response
1	Reflection on Writing Process
1	Reading Log
1	Writing Log

Sample #2

1	Complete Writing Process Package from the first school month, including peer editing and reflection
1	Complete Writing Process Package from the second school month, including peer editing and reflection
1	Reading Log
1	Writing Log

Sample #3

5 Genre Samples:
- Story
- Poem
- Descriptive Essay
- Evaluation Essay
- Biography

2 Reflections on Two of Above Pieces

1 Response to Reading

Sample #4

4 Examples from the Writing Domains:
- Evaluation
- Autobiographical Incident
- Observational Writing
- First-Hand Biography
- Problem Solution
- Report of Information
- Speculation About Causes
- Story

4 Reflections of Writing

Sample #5

1 Writing Sample from each Thematic Unit:
- Animals
- Seasons
- Holidays
- Black Americans
- Careers

2 Quick Writes

1 Reading Log

1 Writing Log

Sample #6

1	Reading Log
2	Writing Log
2	Journal Entries
2	Writing Samples from the beginning of the school year
2	Writing Samples from the end of the school year
1	Reflection on Progress

Math and Science in the Portfolio

Mathematically Powerful Students

Mathematically powerful students are those who can use math to achieve their purposes and then communicate their results.

They achieve their purposes in a variety of ways. They are comfortable with various thinking methods: they can analyze, predict, and verify; they can think about dimension and quantity; they can cope with uncertainly and change. They are well equipped with the techniques and tools of math: they can calculate and compute; they can use concrete material, diagrams, models, and mathematical notation.

They communicate their results through traditional mathematical means — numbers, symbols, graphs, and tables — but more and more they are being encouraged to communicate their results through language, both oral and written.

Math Communications Make Perfect Portfolio Material

These communications—which may take the form of individual projects, math journals, descriptions of difficulties and/or success, as well as essays reflecting on progress and growth — are perfect material for inclusion in a portfolio and a valuable tool in the assessment process.

Science and the Portfolio

A written record of the scientific method in action is also material that is made-to-order for inclusion in the portfolio. The steps lend themselves to almost any grade level and provide student-generated products that will demonstrate growth and progress over a period of time.

- State the problem.

- Gather information.

- State your hypothesis.
  (Make an educated guess.)

- Investigate.
  (Test your hypothesis.)

- Draw a conclusion.
  (Interpret data.)

- Communicate results.
  (Record on graph or chart).

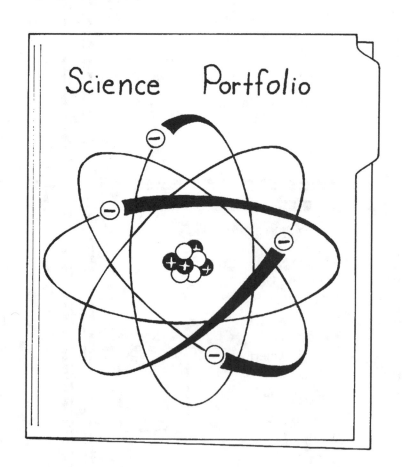

116 ©1995 Teacher Created Materials, Inc.

Reflecting on Progress

This **primary level** form is designed to introduce students to the idea of looking at the progress they have made over a period of time. You will want to discuss the idea and fill in a word or words below to help them know what to look for.

I'm Getting Better and Better!

Name _____

Between_____ and _____,

my work has improved in _____,

_____, and _____.

This is how I feel about my work:

Reflecting on Progress in Writing

*This **upper grade level** form is designed to assist students in reflecting on their general progress in writing. Since reflection tends to be a subjective process, a form is not the ideal vehicle for reflecting on general progress any more than it is ideal for reflecting on a particular piece. However, the form may help to introduce the idea in this area also.*

- -

Reflecting on Progress in Writing

Name _____ Date _____

During _____ my writing improved in
(Circle one or more.)

fluency   **organization**   **creativity**   **clarity**   **mechanics**

This improvement can be noticed because _____

_____

_____

_____

_____ .

During the next _____ ,

I plan to work on _____

_____

_____

_____

_____ .

Reflecting on Progress in Math

*This **upper grade level** form is designed to assist students in reflecting on their general progress in math. Since reflection tends to be a subjective process, a form is not the ideal vehicle for reflecting on general progress anymore than it is ideal for reflecting on a particular piece of work. However, a form may help to introduce the idea in this area also.*

- -

Reflecting on Progress in Math

Name _____ Date _____

During _____, my writing improved in
(Circle one or more.)

estimation   **computation**   **accuracy**   **problem solving**

This improvement can be noticed because _____

_____

_____

_____

_____ .

During the next _____ ,

I plan to work on _____

_____

_____

_____ .

The Reflective Essay—Lesson Plan

Reflections are so important to the development of authentic portfolio assessment that they deserve a separate look. The ability of a student to evaluate his or her own work by taking a thoughtful look at it over a period of time has only recently been discovered and acknowledged. This, at first glance, seems to be a very adult skill. However, students respond well to this challenge. In fact, some of their best writing is done during the process of thoughtful reflection.

Students are asked to reflect on their work when they choose it for their Showcase Portfolios. They are also asked to evaluate their collected writing and reflect on the progress they have made. This second process is a good motivation for a quick write that is really a reflective essay.

A Lesson Plan for a Reflection

This is a whole-class activity. Students should have their Showcase Portfolios at hand.

Inform the students that they will be writing a reflective essays about the progress they have made in writing over a period of time. Tell them that the essay will be a quick write and will go into their Showcase Portfolios.

Introduce the "Writing Situation" by reviewing the aspects of writing that you have stressed during the year so far:

So far this year we have worked on developing fluency, organization, and creativity (or whatever is applicable to your own writing program). We have also edited our writing, using what we know about mechanics: punctuation, capitalization, usage, and spelling.

Give me a definition of fluency, of organization, and creativity. (Brainstorm with the class and write the students' ideas on the board under these classifications. Discuss ideas.)

Write an essay telling how your writing has improved during the first half of this year. Give some examples to support your ideas. Look through your portfolio for ideas. End by telling me the grade you think you deserve for writing.

The Reflective Essay—Teacher Script

Although students can be helped to reflect upon their work by filling out a loosely structured form, the best reflections are written in essay form.

Take time to explain and brainstorm examples of the qualities you want the students to look for in their writing.

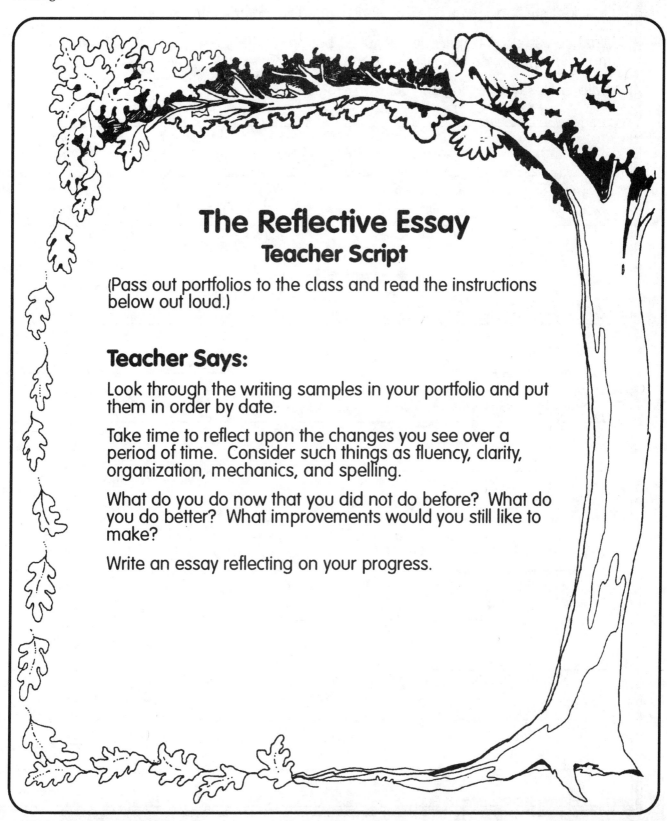

The Reflective Essay
Teacher Script

(Pass out portfolios to the class and read the instructions below out loud.)

Teacher Says:

Look through the writing samples in your portfolio and put them in order by date.

Take time to reflect upon the changes you see over a period of time. Consider such things as fluency, clarity, organization, mechanics, and spelling.

What do you do now that you did not do before? What do you do better? What improvements would you still like to make?

Write an essay reflecting on your progress.

The Reflective Essay—Student Prompt

Look through the writing samples in your portfolio and put them in order by date.

Take time to reflect upon the changes you see over a period of time.

Consider such things as fluency, clarity, organization, mechanics, and spelling.

What do you do now that you did not do before? What do you do better? What improvements would you still like to make?

Write an essay reflecting on your own progress.

_____

_____

_____

_____

_____

_____

_____

_____

_____

_____

_____

_____

_____

_____

_____

Step Five of the Portfolio Planner

The Special, Spectacular Cover

Although you are already "showcasing" when you choose the papers to save in a special portfolio, it probably will not feel official to you or your students until they have had a chance to make a special, spectacular portfolio cover. You can plan and complete this project ahead of time and store the finished covers away for the big moment, or you can have students store the showcase papers they have selected in a special file drawer until they have finished their portfolio covers.

Anything Goes

Since Showcase Portfolios are not meant to be working portfolios, sturdiness and durability are not important requirements. They can be designed in light colors with cut-outs and overlays or any other delicate addition that suits their fancy. These portfolios will not need to be accessible either, since they will be brought out only at special times for special reasons. For that reason the storage of Showcase Portfolios is not usually a problem. They can be stacked on top of a high cupboard or at the back of a deep shelf until they are needed.

Making the Container

The portfolio itself (the container) is usually put together like an artist's portfolio. You can hinge two pieces of heavy tagboard or poster board at the bottom with tape and tie the tops together with cord, string, or ribbon. Consider using wide plastic tape and apply it to both the inside and outside of the bottom edges to make a strong hinge and to avoid any sticky surface that might catch and tear the papers that will go inside. (The sides can also be taped closed, though this makes putting the papers in and taking them out hard to do without damaging everything.) Colorful shoestrings make good strong ties for this kind of portfolio.

You can also choose to use commercially available containers with accordion pleated sides or protective transparent inserts.

Larger Containers

Sometimes the portfolio needs to be larger than a folder. If you want a larger, sturdier portfolio, you might consider starting with a box. This will allow the inclusion of objects such as video and audio tapes, science specimens, models, and so on. The boxes you choose should have sturdy lids that are not difficult to remove. Explore shops that specialize in storage containers or the closet departments of larger stores.

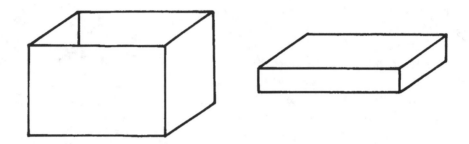

If you are really ambitious you could cut the bottom, sides, and top lid of a box shape out of sturdy corrugated cardboard and tape them together. This would give you the opportunity to create a custom shape for a particular purpose. A box like this could be covered with wallpaper or contact paper which would help to hold it together as well as provide a surface for the application of decoration.

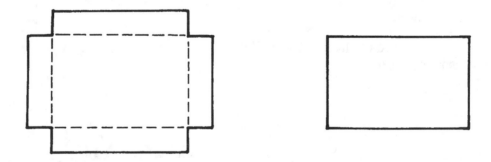

Adding the Art

However you decide to make (or buy) your containers, you will want to add art as a decorative statement to one or both outside covers. If you start with two pieces of tagboard or poster board that you plan to tape together, you can create your art directly on the surfaces before you join them. If you are using some other kind of folder or a box, you will need to create your artistic product on another piece of paper and attach it to the outside of the portfolio. There are many kinds of glues available in hobby or craft stores to help you with this process.

If you would like to add a protective covering to the surface of the finished portfolio, consider spraying it with an acrylic spray or covering it with a sheet of clear contact paper.

Name Stencils and Patterns

Materials:

- Punch-out letters in different styles (from your favorite teacher supply store)
- Poster paints in assorted colors
- Flat pans
- Small paint rollers (from a hobby or craft store)
- Medium and small paint brushes
- Pens, pencils, scissors, etc.

Method:

Punch out the letters carefully, keeping the frames intact. Trim the frames to a uniform size.

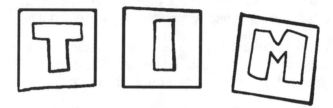

Have students make designs based on their own names by tracing around the different styles of letters and filling them in with paint

or by making the letter frames into stencils of their names and rolling paint across them.

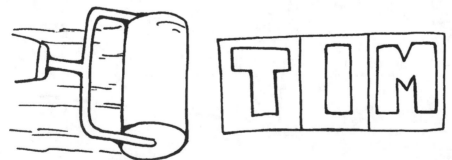

You may want students to spend several days on this project because special effects can be obtained by letting the paint dry and repainting with another color.

Head Map Collages

Materials:

- Silhouette patterns in profile, representing various hairstyles and facial types for students to choose from

- Poster board or paper and assorted art supplies, including scissors and glue or dry-mount spray

- Stacks of old magazines to cut up

Method:

Have each student choose a pattern and trace it on his or her poster board or paper.

Decide ahead of time with the class the areas that will be represented in the head map. Will it contain everything the student is interested in, or will it reflect just the contents of the portfolio? You could have both kinds—one on the back and one on the front. Or you could have one representing school interests and one representing out-of-school activities.

Show the students how to cut around shapes to prepare them for use in a collage. Have them experiment with placement before attaching things permanently. Consider using dry-mount spray that allows you to peel things off and move them around.

Don't forget to have students put their names on their portfolios.

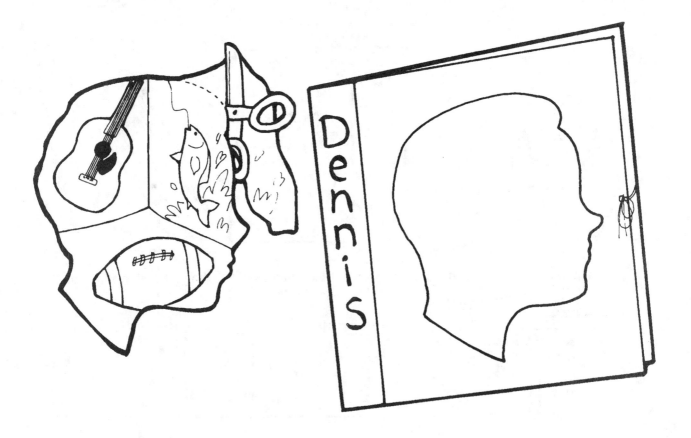

Coat of Arms or Shield

Much the same idea can be expressed in a shield or coat of arms. Enlarge the drawing below to make patterns for the students to trace.

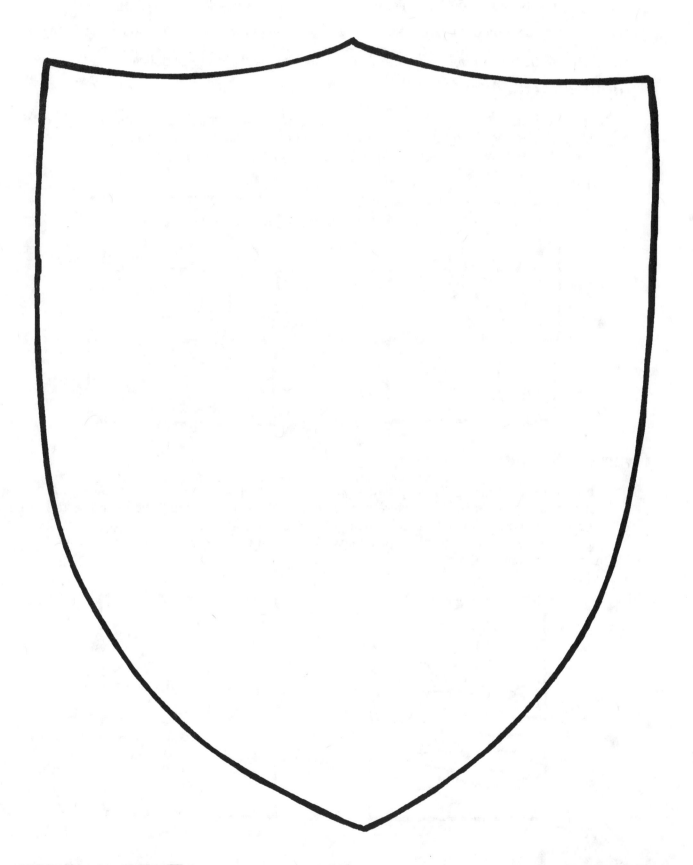

Paper Sculptures and Overlays

Materials:

- Assorted colors of construction paper

- Scissors, glue, pencils, etc. (craft knives for students who are old enough to handle them)

- Large plastic bags to store the portfolios in since they will tend to be delicate

Sculpture Method:

In this project, students can let their imaginations run wild. Paper can be torn or cut precisely. Any kind of scene or object can be built up. You might want to make a sample or two to get your students started, or you may wish to leave them entirely on their own.

Overlay Method:

This cut-paper project consists of two separate parts—a picture to form the foundation and a cut paper design go over it. The picture can be created especially for the project, or a picture from a unit in the portfolio can be used. The cut-paper overlay should go with the theme of the picture and the portfolio or could just consist of cut-out letters spelling the name of the portfolio's theme and the student's name.

Spatter and Blow

Materials:

- Paper (Don't try this directly on your portfolio.)

- Poster paints in a variety of colors

- Window screening set into small frames (You can use embroidery hoops.)

- Old toothbrushes

- Paintbrushes

- Drinking straws

Spatter Method:

(Have students put their names on the backs of their papers before they begin.) Dip toothbrush in paint. Tap off excess paint. Draw brush across screening held over paper. Try several different colors.

Experiment until you get it the way you want it. This is not as easy as it sounds, and you will want to let each student make several attempts.

Let all the paintings dry completely. They will not be smooth and flat. When all are dry, stack them and pile heavy books on them for several days. When they are smooth and flat, attach them to the outside surfaces of the portfolios.

Blow Method:

(Have students put their names on the backs of their papers before they begin.) Dip a paintbrush in one color and drip some paint on the paper. Blow gently through a straw to make the paint spread and run. Repeat with several different colors but stop before it gets muddy-looking.

Let each student make several attempts. It takes a while to get the hang of it. Dry and press as described above.

Showcasing

Materials:

- Paper

- Crayons, paintbrushes, scrapers (craft sticks, paper clips, rulers, etc.)

- Thick black poster paint, thin washes of blue or white poster paint

Scratch-Off Method:

Have students cover their papers with a design done in heavy crayon. They can use one color or many colors but the whole paper should be covered.

Use a brush to apply thick black poster paint to the paper, completely covering the crayon.

When the paint is dry, use a scraper to remove the black paint to make a design or picture. Black silhouettes against a sunset sky are very effective, as are fireworks.

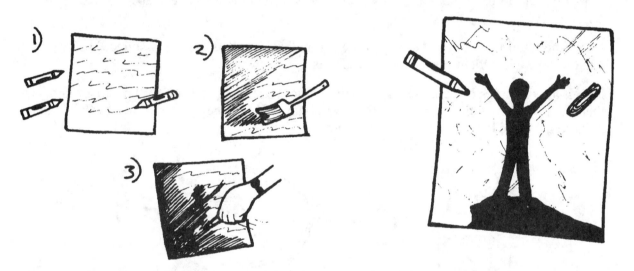

Crayon-Resist Method:

Draw a picture, using crayons. Underwater scenes and winter scenes are effective.

Apply a thin wash of blue paint for an underwater effect or of white paint for snow.

Stamping

Materials:

- Drawing paper
- Scratch paper
- Poster paint and paper towels

Things to stamp with:

- fruits such as oranges, apples, lemons, etc., cut to expose a textured surface
- potatoes, cut and carved with implements such as plastic knives and forks
- sponges, cut into shapes such as fish, bugs, flowers, etc.
- cookie cutters
- rubber erasers

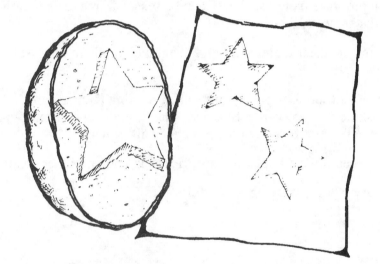

Method:

Have students write their names on the backs of their papers before beginning to paint.

Dip surface of "stamper" into poster paint. Press on paper towel to remove excess paint. Stamp on paper.

Students can use different colors and different stampers to create a variety of designs. Allow time to experiment with designs on scratch paper before creating a final design for the portfolio cover.

Allow designs to dry thoroughly. Then stack them and place heavy books on the stack for several days to flatten the papers before attaching designs to the portfolios.

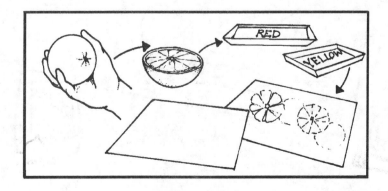

Cut-and-Glue Fabric Applique

Materials:

- Drawing paper or colored construction paper

- Scissors, pencils

- Glue that works on fabric and paper and will dry clear

- Scraps of fabric, lace, rickrack, etc.

- Patterns for appropriate shapes (See page 133 for patterns and suggestions.)

Method:

Choose appropriate patterns. These can be seasonal, matched to a theme, or simply appealing to you and the students.

Lay patterns on material, trace around them, and cut them out. Start with just a few and cut more as desired.

Lay pieces of material on the writing paper, moving them around, adding more, and combining colors until the composition is finished. The design can consist of one central motif or of repeated smaller motifs, giving the effect of quilt squares.

Glue the pieces down. Trim with lace, rickrack, and any other desired trim.

Allow to dry before attaching to portfolio.

132
©1995 Teacher Created Materials, Inc.

Cut-and-Glue Fabric Applique *(cont.)*

Sample Patterns

Use the sample patterns on this page for seasonal cut-and-glue appliques. You can find others by searching through coloring books designed for small children. These simple outline drawings lend themselves to this kind of craft.

Geometric Shapes

Materials:

- Drawing paper

- Paints (poster paints, acrylics, watercolors) in clear, bright colors

- Pencils, rulers, paintbrushes

- Shiny black tape, 1/4" (.6 cm) wide

Method:

Display one or more samples of Piet Mondrian's work. He painted compositions based on geometric shapes such as rectangles, using mostly primary colors and white. His shapes are bordered in straight black lines, giving an effect like a very modern stained glass window.

Have students use pencils and rulers to draw rectangles of various sizes, covering the whole paper. Some of the rectangles should be painted in clear, bright colors while some are left white. (Mondrian used primary colors, but violet, purple, turquoise, green, and bright pink are also very effective.)

When the paint is completely dry, students should edge their rectangles with narrow black tape. Attach the completed designs to the portfolio covers.

These portfolios make a beautiful Open House display, especially when they are laid flat on all the individual desk tops in a classroom.

Pointillism

Materials:

- Drawing paper
- Pencils
- Art gum erasers
- Paint and brushes or fineline markers

Method:

Display one or more samples of Georges Seurat's work and discuss pointillism, the art technique in which tiny dots of color are placed side by side.

Have students draw pictures or designs that are appropriate for the season, your theme, or to meet some other criteria. These pictures should be drawn very lightly and shaded in with color applied in tiny dots.

When the paint or ink is completely dry, all pencil lines should be erased.

The finished product of this technique can be very beautiful, and some people really enjoy the process of applying tiny dots of color. Nevertheless, it can be frustrating to those who prefer to work in big, bold strokes of color, so you may wish to offer an alternative art project for them.

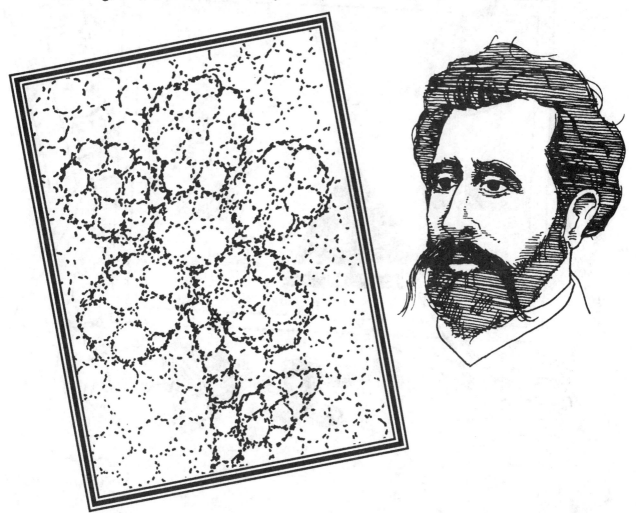

Materials:

- Drawing paper, black construction paper
- Watercolors, brushes
- Scissors, pencils, glue
- Patterns (see pages 137 and 138)

Method:

Students should cover entire paper with a wash in sunset colors—yellows, oranges, reds.

Allow paint to dry and then glue on silhouettes that have been cut from black construction paper. Students can use their imaginations to create their own silhouettes or trace and cut out figures from the patterns on pages 137 and 138.

Sample Patterns

Step Six of the Portfolio Planner

Built-In Uses

Some ways of using portfolios are built in. They come with the territory.

- Showcase Portfolios constitute a ready-made display of progress for Open House. You do not have to do anything except one last sorting process.

- Showcase Portfolios also serve as a record of progress to be sent home with each student at the end of the school year.

- Best of all, Showcase Portfolios will have provided during the whole school year—along with the Collection Portfolios they are drawn from—a technique for allowing students to take ownership of the learning process. You will have given them the gift of monitoring their own work and reflecting on their own progress over time.

The Showcase Portfolio as an Assessment Tool

Since the Showcase Portfolio has already been sorted and preselected to show progress over a period of time and to represent the criteria on which you and the students have collaborated, both the work samples contained in the portfolios and the criteria statement itself will lay a foundation for assessment.

You will also have the benefit of the reflections written by the students about the pieces and about general growth and progress. If you have chosen to include peer-editing statements, you will have that feedback as well.

In short, you will be in a position to have not only an overview and a general feeling of progress but also a good idea of appropriate grades and the materials to back up your decisions. This is a wonderful asset when you are conferring about grades with parents.

New Assessments—Old Report Cards

In spite of the fact that you may be using portfolio assessment as part of your district's or your school's policy, you may still be faced with filling in the old report cards that were designed to show grades based on averages and percentages. There are a couple of easy ways of dealing with this:

- Make mental adjustments when you compute your grades, giving more weight to grades at the end of the grading period than at the beginning in order to reflect the progress that was made over time.

- In order to emphasize the importance of portfolio assessment in your program, make a form like the one on the next page a part of your report card package.

This form can accompany the regular report card to formalize the part played by the portfolio in the student's assessment.

ABCDEFGHIJKLMNOPQRSTUVWXYZ

Parent Conference Form
❖ ❖ ❖ ❖ ❖
Portfolio Assessment

Date: _____

Student's Name: _____

Contents of Portfolio

Assignment	Completed	Degree of Success

_____   _____
        Parent   *Teacher*

Step Seven of the Portfolio Planner

Get on Your Mark

Make sure that you have read the first six steps of portfolio planning and browsed through the forms that accompany them.

Reproduce as many pages of the blank calendar on page 144 as you will need for your school year (or use a commercial calendar). Some people like to enlarge the calendar squares to allow more room for making notes.

Look at the sample calendar on pages 142 and 143. The first four months of a traditional school year have been modeled for you.

Get Set

With a regular calendar and a list of school events in front of you, mark all of the vacations, school holidays, religious holidays, inservice meeting days, school-related rehearsals and celebrations, conference periods, and anything else you can think of. Check the way this has been done on the sample calendar months.

Now, working backwards, you will know at a glance that you should have your first round of Showcase Portfolios (both the sorted papers and the spectacular covers) completed at least a week before the first conference period (12/6–12/8). Looking at the time realistically, you might pass out the Collection Portfolios to start the sorting process on November 21 and 22. After the long Thanksgiving weekend, the students can look over their sorted papers and write reflections on their progress. They can make their portfolio covers November 30 through December 2, leaving you with a weekend to finish making out report cards and getting ready to confer with parents. (If your first conference period is earlier or later, be sure to make adjustments.)

Go

Still working backwards, decide how many thematic units or writing process cycles you can complete between the beginning of school and "Sorting Day" on November 21. You will have between 45 and 46 days or an average of about nine weeks. Call it eight real weeks to be on the safe side and allow for two thematic units or four cycles of the writing process. Mark your Completion Days. You can call them WS (for writing samples) and Theme. (See sample calendars.) Those are the days that all of the papers representing that Writing Sample or Theme must be in the portfolios. Students (or your Portfolio Aides) will be putting them in the portfolios as they go along.

Win

Working with this kind of a calendar skeleton, you can plan ahead, even during the summer, and be all set to go when school starts. Make or buy the folders for your Collection Portfolios. Label them with names if you can get your class list ahead of time. Decide where you are going to store them and then put them there. When school starts, you will be able to spend your valuable time on your curriculum and on facilitating the portfolio process for your students.

September
Month 1

M	Tu	W	Th	F
			1	2
5 Labor Day	Teachers' 6 Meetings Rosh Hashanah	7	8 School Starts	9
12	13	14	15 Yom Kippur	16
19	20 Sukkoth	21	22	23 WS – 1
26	27	28	29	30

October
Month 2

M	Tu	W	Th	F
3	4	5	6	7 WS – 2
10 Columbus Day	11	12	13	14
17	18	19	20	21 WS – 3
24	25	26	27 All-School Field Day	28
31 Halloween				

Calendar Model *(cont.)*

November
Month 3

M	Tu	W	Th	F
	1	2	3	4
7	8 Election Day	9	10 Veterans Day	11 Veterans Day
14	15	16	17	18 WS – 4 Theme - 2
21 Sort Papers	22 Sort Papers	23 Student Council Crazy Day	24 Thanksgiving	25
Write 28 Reflections Hanukkah Begins	29 Write Reflections	30 Make Covers		

December
Month 4

M	Tu	W	Th	F
			1 Make Covers	2
5 Hanukkah Ends	6 1st Conference Period	7 1st Conference Period	8 1st Conference Period	9
12	13 Rehearsals	14	15	16 Holiday Program
19	20 Winter	21	22	23
26 / 31 Holiday				

F

Th

W

Tu

M

144

©1995 Teacher Created Materials, Inc.